SHAPED in REDEMPTION
to Live Life's Greatest Adventure

*How God accepts us, grows us, calls us,
keeps us and what it means in daily life*

DAVID C. PEQUEÑO

Shaped in Redemption to Live Life's Greatest Adventure
How God accepts us, grows us, calls us, keeps us and what it means in daily life
by David C. Pequeño

Printed in the United States of America.

ISBN 9781498439893

www.xulonpress.com

I dedicate this book to my
beloved son Jonathan
and for the building up of
God's people in His amazing
REDEMPTION.

To the men and women behind the fence
who encouraged me to write

I wish to thank Brad Hall and Jennifer Omaña
for assisting in the initial editing.

CONTENTS

Introduction

Life's Normal Expectations

If you are like the majority, you probably have a natural inclination to expect good outcomes in life. Truth is, everybody wants to be a winner in life. I have never known anyone with the desire to fail or to settle for less in life. I have never heard a coach say to his players, "Okay guys, this is the big one. We've worked real hard to get here; now let's go out and lose this one for the fans," followed by pumped-up players chanting, "Lose, lose, lose!" It would be extremely uncommon to hear the groom and the bride exchange their vows ending in the clergy saying; "I now pronounce you husband and wife, may you live happily ever after until divorce do ye part." Although traditional marriage vows have these statements about "for richer or poorer, in sickness and in health," truth is, newlyweds never enter marriage expecting gloom and doom. We all enter marriage with the expectation of mutual lifelong fulfillment. Life to the fullest extent is what we all assume is the norm, and even when things go wrong we never accept it as normal. Perhaps this is the implication in abnormal psychology. By human expectation, it is not normal when bad things happen to people.

Jesus Himself said that He had come to give life and to give it more abundantly. If in no other area of life are we willing to agree with His authority, it would be difficult to find anyone disagreeing with His sentiment about abundant life. We all anticipate a good life that is the normal expectation in every human being. Nevertheless, it should be noted that in the same breath Jesus willed abundant life, He also said the thief comes to steal, kill, and destroy (John 10:10). Our Lord Jesus must have been extremely familiar with the human condition and genuinely interested in our greatest well-being to make such a precise statement about human life.

Yes, it's true—every human wants to thrive in what matters most in life, but the reality is that we live in a fallen world, we have a fallen nature, and we live under the influence of a fallen creature who seeks to devour us like a lion devours its prey (1 Peter 5:8). Jesus Christ did not try to hide or minimize the human predicament; in fact, He came to invade our darkness with His glorious light.

> Giving thanks to the Father who has qualified us to be
> partakers of the inheritance of the saints in the light.
> He has delivered us from the power of darkness and
> conveyed us into the kingdom of the Son of His love,
> in whom we have redemption through His blood, the
> forgiveness of sins.   Colossians 1:12–14

The words of Jesus Christ are what draw me in. Knowing the odds are heavily against us, He promises abundant life. Perhaps the reason we don't experience more of the abundant life Jesus promised is that when we start planning for a great life, we usually begin with our preferences. Not that our preferences are wrong in themselves— however, life's ultimate planning question should not begin with our likes or dislikes. Life's ultimate question comes down to essence, who are we at the core of our being? This is by far the better place to begin when asking questions about greater life fulfillment. The reason being is that we cannot live in contradiction to our true self and live consistently well, at least not for the duration of a life time. There is pleasure in sin, no doubt, but it is short lived. Perhaps the reason we miss out on the abundant life Christ desires for all His children is that the teaching of redemption has been limited to only a message of forgiveness and the hope of heaven, but with very little emphasis on what happens in between forgiveness and heaven. In other words, redemption has a great beginning and a great ending, but no real great in between.

Please do not misunderstand my intentions. I am fully aware and on board with man's primary need for forgiveness and a restored relationship with his Creator God. This is indeed the greatest truth of the gospel. Nevertheless, I am deeply concerned with the current practice in Christendom and the negative implication it has on the gospel of Jesus Christ. In today's world, it is not uncommon for Christians to hear the gospel on Sunday morning followed by a Monday morning session with their therapist.

The need to have a pastor guide us in the context of church life and a therapist to guide us in the context of everyday life issues, implies the gospel of Jesus Christ is impotent to speak life into our growth needs. I am not against counseling having a background in counseling myself, nor am I promoting an anti-counseling agenda. However, I do see the need to address this growing practice, since the danger in this type of Christianity is that it puts into question the efficacy of the gospel.

The logical progression in this current practice is to question the role the gospel plays in everyday life. Why do I need to hear the preacher or the Sunday school teacher when it is my therapist who is helping me gain greater life-awareness? While it is true that the gospel at its core is about the forgiveness of sin, it is also true that the forgiveness of sin is not the graduation of Christian life. In reality, it is only the beginning of your God adventure.

The idea that the gospel has little relevance in between forgiveness and heaven has created a generation of Christians who can't explain their own Christianity, nor can they explain why their beliefs work in real life situations. The catch all answer of those who have been brought up under the influence of intimidation and fear theology is that God's smoking gun is aimed and ready to punish all disobedience at first sight. Fear theology has made Christians paranoid of life and paranoid of their God; simply because the primary goal in fear theology is to avoid consequences, rather than to grow in the understanding that the God of absolute power, the Creator of heaven and earth, is also our heavenly Father too through Jesus Christ. Contrary to the popular teaching in fear theology, God's first thought towards us is not condemnation, but rather redemption and restoration leading to life's greatest adventure.

> This is how much God loved the world: He gave his Son, his one and only Son. And this is why: so that no one need be destroyed; by believing in him, anyone can have a whole and lasting life. God didn't go to all the trouble of sending his Son merely to point an accusing finger, telling the world how bad it was. He came to help, to put the world right again. Anyone who trusts in him is acquitted; anyone who refuses to trust him has long since been under the death sentence without knowing it.   John 3:16–18 MSG

In chapter 1 of his second epistle, the apostle Peter said that through God's power we have been given all things that pertain to life and godliness (2 Peter 1:3). In light of this great truth, he encourages us to be diligent in this calling by realigning our lives to what is true of us through the gospel, rather than what is true of us from the experiences of a fallen world.

Specifically he says that we are to add to our faith: virtue, knowledge, self-control, perseverance, godliness, brotherly kindness, and love (2 Peter 1:5–7). It is obvious that what Peter had in mind is the life that is lived between forgiveness and heaven. In the verses that follow, he says that if we live out our calling we will never stumble (2 Peter 1:10).

I find it remarkable that the issues Peter brings up concerning life development are the same ones that would be brought up in a counseling session with your therapist. Becoming a Christian and punching your ticket into eternity happens in the moment of faith in Jesus Christ, but becoming an effective Christian requires intentional learning. Additionally, we must know that it cannot be possible that the message of the gospel is limited to only a great beginning and a great ending, but with no real great in between. It would be unrealistic to believe that God who gave us His Son at the cross to make the past right and assure us of a glorious future, would have nothing to say about life in the present.

It should be noted through the New Testament that God is very much interested in our personal life development. The New Testament is made up of twenty-seven books. The first four—Matthew, Mark, Luke and John—are known as the Synoptic Gospels. These four Gospels record the life history of Jesus Christ; with His life, death, and resurrection being the central focus. This is the *heart* of the gospel. The book of Acts records the coming of the Holy Spirit and the expansion of the gospel through the evangelistic outreach of Christ's disciples. This is the *work* of the gospel. The last book in the New Testament, the book of Revelation is about the second coming of Christ, when God will restore all things to His original intent. This is the *victory* of the gospel. The books between Acts and Revelation are twenty-one books, and they were written for the purpose of understanding the gospel and for our personal life growth and development. This is the *fulfillment* of the gospel.

As one can easily conclude, the math is not difficult to see; four books written to reveal the life of Jesus Christ, one book to record the work of the gospel, one book to reveal the future victory of the gospel, and twenty-one books written on Christian life growth and development. Does God care about our personal growth and life development? My guess would be, yes! Nevertheless, many churches still continue to delegate personal life-growth issues to other entities outside of the gospel. In other words, the gospel has the power to save us, but apparently not the power to grow us.

Personal-life development must be sought elsewhere according to the limited version of the gospel, and it's what keeps the therapist's number on speed dial. Nevertheless, such should not be the case. The gospel is intensely relevant and meaningful to every significant activity under the sun. However, if we continue to remain indifferent towards teaching the all-inclusive message of the gospel with emphasis on life growth leading to our kingdom purpose, the message we are indirectly communicating to a generation that is searching for meaning and purpose is that God's message is irrelevant to real-life issues.

For this reason, it is necessary to take a fresh look at how the gospel impacts the total human experience. What influence do justification, sanctification, calling, and glorification have on daily life and what is the connection to the abundant life Jesus promised? I fear that the fundamental truths of our redemption have lost their relevance and influence in the everyday mechanics of real life. A gospel that is able to save us from eternal judgment but not able to speak life into our daily concerns is not the gospel Jesus Christ left us. In interpreting the whole impact God's truth has on the quality of life, with the gospel of Jesus Christ being the climax of His revelation Paul said:

> The whole Bible was given to us by inspiration from God and is useful to teach us what is true and to make us realize what is wrong in our lives; it straightens us out and helps us do what is right. It is God's way of making us well prepared at every point, fully equipped to do good to everyone.   2 Timothy 3:16–17 TLB

Chapter 1

The Incredible Shrinking Christian

D oes anyone believe God has anything to do with how life turns out anymore? Obviously, for the atheist and agnostic, there is considerable doubt that God has anything to do with anything good and positive. What is surprisingly odd is that even in the Christian community, God seems to be on the outside looking in.

Truth be known, all human existence revolves around two life endeavors. We are either on a life journey where we are trying to reinvent ourselves on the basis of what the material world has to offer. Or we are on a path in life where we are rediscovering our authentic selves on the basis of having been created in the image of God, two different pursuits with enormous differences in the outcome of life. You can rest assured that the spiritual dimension of our lives isn't going away anytime soon. It is an essential part in the totality of what it means to be truly human.

We are either on a life journey where we are trying to reinvent ourselves on the basis of what the material world has to offer, or we are on a path in life where we are rediscovering our authentic selves

Unfortunately when it comes to the spiritual dimension of our lives, it is often ignored, overlooked, or becomes mysteriously spooky or destructive.

We have all seen how unhealthy spirituality works in the lives of people who crash planes into buildings believing they are doing the will of God, or people who brainwash other human beings into being nothing more than objects of manipulation. We have all been shocked by the massive suicides conducted by religious leaders proclaiming to be God's special messengers. Unfortunately, in a fallen world where good and evil coexist; acts of inhumanity committed under the banner of religious authority will continue to shock the world. Perhaps the greatest harm done by these misguided religious fanatics is the negative influence they have on people who are becoming more suspicious and indifferent toward authentic spirituality.

In our minds, we should never lose sight of the truth the angels proclaimed at the birth of Christ: "Glory to God in the highest, and on earth peace, goodwill toward men" (Luke 2:14). Authentic spirituality was never intended to be mysteriously spooky, destructive, or irrelevant to everyday life; being created

Authentic spirituality was never intended to be mysteriously spooky, destructive, or irrelevant to everyday life.

in the image of God means that through Him we know the truth about our origin, our identity, our potential, and ultimately our destiny. The very things that make life worth living and give it meaning and direction are all wrapped up in who we are spiritually.

The spiritual dimension of our lives cannot be ignored or deemed a nonessential preference. It is an integral part of a growing healthy personality. Without it life remains incomplete, along with a deep emptiness and disorientation that nothing in the material world can fill. Spirituality, however is not something we make up as we go through life. Rather, spirituality is something we already are; therefore, it must be rediscovered, not reinvented. For life to be lived out of its greatest potential, it must be anchored in something that is bigger than life itself. To grasp this truth without the influence of toxic theology, it is necessary to give ourselves a fresh start by allowing our perception of God to stand alone on what He has revealed about Himself through Scripture, rather than from our experiences with religious fanatics.

The Origin of Mankind

In Genesis, God creates Adam and Eve in His own image. Being created in the image of God would obviously mean that their significance and meaning in life would revolve around their relationship with God. Why would God create humans with the ability to intelligently relate to Him and not engage them in any significant manner? Their whole lives were designed to be lived in a meaningful dependent relationship with God.

> So God created man in His own image; in the image
> of God He created him; male and female He created
> them. Then God blessed them, and God said to them,
> "Be fruitful and multiply; fill the earth and subdue it;
> have dominion over the fish of the sea, over the birds
> of the air, and over every living thing that moves on
> the earth." Genesis 1:27–28

In Genesis, God made Adam and Eve the rulers of earth. All would be in submission to them making them the crown of creation. They would lord over creation and God would be Lord over them.

17

His lordship over Adam and Eve would not be strenuous, hard, or difficult. He would not rule over them with an iron fist. God would be their Lord in Paradise with all their needs more than adequately met and with nothing left to be desired. However, to validate His lordship over Adam and Eve, God instituted one prohibition—only one.

Notice that there would not be many ways in which Adam and Eve could come into conflict with their maker, thus reducing obedience to a bare minimal effort. In the land of good and plenty, there was only one thing Adam and Eve needed to remember. They were not to eat of the fruit of the tree of the knowledge of good and evil. It was the easiest open-book test to pass in several ways.

First, it was visible. Adam and Eve did not have to worry about the possibility of one day accidentally eating from the wrong tree. That simply could not occur since it had been singled out to them. Second, the bountiful comfort and secure living they enjoyed at the cost of God's grace and goodness would have eliminated any motivation for revolt. They didn't need to fix or improve anything in the garden of Paradise. Third, the knowledge of good and evil would have been a nonissue since God Himself, the Alpha and Omega, was their reference point to all that could possibly be known. Finally, the one single prohibition carried with it the severest of consequences; death. Adam and Eve must have been educated by God Himself as to the meaning of death for it to serve as a deterrent.

Satan, however through his persistence was finally able to convince God's creatures created in His image to commit high treason. Eve was convinced that the very thing that was forbidden was actually the one thing she needed above all else to become more like God. She ate of the forbidden fruit as did her husband Adam. In retrospect, this was a rather odd craving for Eve and Adam, since they were already in similarity to God having been created in His image. The knowledge of good and evil that was forbidden for them to know was to have knowledge equal to God, but without the ability to use it for the highest possible good as only the self-existing all-powerful God could do.

In Genesis there was a Creator, and the Creator created Adam and Eve in His image. Being created in the image of God so that their meaning and purpose in life would revolve around knowing Him was the best thing that could have happened for created beings. But to believe that the created beings could actually share equality with God was sure death, just as God had warned Adam and Eve. We were created in the image of God, but that doesn't make us share equality with Him.

Centuries later the apostle Paul described the Genesis factor in his own life as he wrote to the Christians in Rome. Paul said in Romans chapter 7 that he knew the difference between good and evil, that was not his problem. His problem, as he admitted was that he didn't have the willpower in his flesh to do the good he knew to do, nor did he have the willpower to avoid the evil he knew not to do.

> For I know that in me (that is, in my flesh) nothing good dwells; for to will is present with me, but how to perform what is good I do not find. For the good that I will to do, I do not do; but the evil I will not to do, that I practice. Romans 7:18–19

This is the human dilemma even to the current time we live in. There is no need to live in denial, the truth is in our own behavior. We have all been in situations where we knew the right thing to do, but still ended up doing what we knew in our hearts was wrong. Sigmund

Freud called it an "internal struggle" that goes on inside every man between the id, ego, and superego. Carl Jung acknowledged a "dark shadow" that exists in every human being. Carl Rogers said we are all "fallible human beings," and Albert Ellis believed all humans have an "irrational side" to their nature. While the earliest psychology theorists and later ones agree that man is in conflict with himself, none have been able to tell us why humans are caught in this dilemma. The only thing they have been able to do is reaffirm biblical truth.

> For all have sinned and fall short of the glory of God. Romans 3:23

Paul had the knowledge of good and evil as did Adam and Eve; as did our ancestors, and as we also have, but it has not resulted in our becoming more like God as Satan promised Eve. On the contrary, in Romans chapter 3, Paul gives an indictment on the human race who also had the knowledge of good and evil. What the apostle Paul makes perfectly clear in the text is that having

Human beings, in spite of knowing the difference between good and evil, cannot consistently convert right head knowledge into right behavior.

the knowledge of good and evil has not resulted in our becoming more like God. The only thing it has resulted in is our becoming more and more unlike God. Human beings, in spite of knowing the difference between good and evil, cannot consistently convert right head knowledge into right behavior. This is what it means to be in a fallen state and separated from God. This is why God commanded Adam and Eve not to eat from the tree of the knowledge of good and evil. But more importantly, this reveals why we need the redemption God provides for us through His Son, Jesus Christ.

In the Genesis account, as it turns out, the one prohibition given to Adam and Eve in the garden was not to restrict potential, as Satan suggested, but rather to protect and preserve potential. After the fall, both Adam and Eve began to experience the problems connected with their separation from God. Death began its slow process of decay, both spiritually and physically. Where once before everything in the created order was in subjection to them it now threatened their very existence.

The Struggle to Believe God in a Broken World

The devastation of the fall, having to adjust from living in a perfect environment to a world where everything was broken, did not create a crisis of belief for Adam and Eve. They did not stop believing in God, nor did they curse and blame God for what went wrong. Their faith was not extinguished nor diminished by the enormous challenges they now faced. Instead, what probably occurred was that Adam and Eve's perspective in life was strengthened. If they had been deceived into doubting the truth and the goodness of God, they now understood clearly beyond a shadow of a doubt, who was truly the lover of their souls and who came disguised as friend to steal, kill, and destroy.

For the rest of us who were born after Genesis 3, our reference point in life doesn't include the experience of Paradise as it did for Adam and Eve. Our reference point in life begins in a broken world. We hear of a God who is all-loving and all-powerful, but for the most part, all we experience is all-suffering.

For the rest of us who were born after Genesis 3, our reference point in life doesn't include the experience of Paradise

The inconsistency of a God who is all-loving and all-powerful in the midst of a world that is all-broken creates a crisis of belief for many who see life without a reference to God's original intent. How can God be all-loving and all-powerful and the world be in disarray? This is an argument of the atheist. If God were all-loving, He would want to stop all the pain and suffering in the world. If God were all-powerful, He could stop all the suffering in the world. Suffering and pain exist in the world. Therefore, God must be all-loving but not all-powerful, or God must be all-powerful but doesn't care to do anything about relieving human suffering. Perhaps He doesn't even exist at all. This reasoning at the very least diminishes the God of Scripture.

The inconsistency of a God who is all-loving and all-powerful in the midst of a world that is all-broken creates a crisis of belief for many

Truth Matters Where Suffering Is the Greatest

The truth you live by determines the quality and hope of your life. Life and death are in the truth you stand by; therefore, it is imperative that your truth stand the test of life's most challenging questions: What is life? What is man? What is history? Where is it going? What is death? What is ethics? Smart people don't just drift through life, they want good answers to life's difficult questions. If the world is broken rather than just accepting it as such, smart people at least want to know why it's broken. Even if we can't fix it, at least it creates a lens of understanding and resolve. In the Christian worldview, sin is an essential factor in understanding the suffering we all experience in a fallen world. However, the concept of sin and redemption is usually not an acceptable option in a society that places great value on the self-made man. Nevertheless, while all might not agree with the biblical interpretation of life, all agree that there is something wrong with the self-destructive behavior man brings upon himself and others.

In fact, the birth and goal of psychology was to present an alternative to the biblical explanation of life. However, as we have already noted, the answers provided by the earliest founders of psychology have not given us options that are entirely different from the biblical account. Even the cognitive restructuring mania that dominates the self-help psychology literature at your local bookstore, cannot claim complete independence from what Jesus Christ taught.

> And you shall know the truth, and the truth shall make
> you free.   John 8:32

Apparently, Jesus Christ Himself believed in cognitive restructuring, as did the apostle Paul who said it was necessary to renew the mind from toxic thinking. It is interesting to note, however, that any concept of human abnormality cannot stand alone. If something is deemed abnormal in the way humans live, there must be a universal standard by which the abnormal is measured; otherwise, it makes absolutely no sense to speak of anything as abnormal.

If something is deemed abnormal in the way humans live, there must be a universal standard by which the abnormal is measured

The abnormal diagnosis in psychological practice cannot exist without some idea of what is normal. However, the sin factor that is fundamental in understanding life from a biblical worldview is offensive in a world where everyone wants to own their own morality; that is, until something gets stolen from them. From this point, morality isn't each man making his own rules to live by. You call the police because it's wrong, and you demand justice. It is very unlikely that you would agree that there is nothing wrong with stealing. I hardly believe you would be okay with the idea that stealing is just another code of morality that happens to be different from yours. I can hardly believe you would be sympathetic with the one who stole your prized possessions in an effort to be more accepting and tolerant in the melting pot of worldviews. If you carry this absurdity to its logical conclusion, life becomes extremely chaotic, and in the end loses its meaning. Perhaps the commandment "thou shall not steal" makes sense after all. Maybe, just maybe, all ten commandments provide a logical foundation on which a healthy social order can be sustained, where we can all live and work together for the common good of all.

Hope and Absurdity

At this point, there is a critical question that needs to be addressed; why pursue a relationship with God in the first place does it really matter? What does faith in God bring to the big picture of life? Do we really need Him, and can we trust Him in the everyday mechanics of life? Is there a significant difference between being a people of faith and non-faith? Is it true as we read in the hymn: "every day with Jesus is sweeter than the day before?"

If the God of the Bible doesn't really exist, then the answer to why pursue a relationship with God is absurd. However, at the same time, the removal of God from the human experience doesn't necessarily usher in an age of liberation and enlightenment. On the contrary, it creates a much greater problem, the problem of self-worship. All of life is experienced from a competitive arena in which the only goal in life is the preservation of self in a world that cannot explain its own existence, cannot explain its own brokenness, nor can it give any real hope of fixing itself. All that can be pursued in life is limited to what is here and now; all the resources to meet life's challenges and disappointments cannot exceed beyond human strength and reason. Life's meaning and purpose are reduced to a survival of the fittest. Hope and destiny at best become a life ritual of eat, drink, and be merry for tomorrow we die.

Creation Without a Creator

In Paul's letter written to the Christians at Rome, he clearly reveals why self-worship creates the greatest threat to personal well-being and social development. In the first chapter, he describes the deterioration of the self-made man as a process that begins when human intellect reasons for a creation

self-worship creates the greatest threat to personal well-being and social development

without a creator. Humanity comes to believe they can trust their own intellect over the sovereign eternal God.

> Although they knew God, they did not glorify Him as God, nor were thankful, but became futile in their thoughts, and their foolish hearts were darkened. Professing to be wise, they became fools.
>
> Romans 1:21–22

For clarification, we must acknowledge that human intellect was not given so that we would remain ignorant and disoriented in life. After all, we were created in the image of an intelligent God in whom are hidden all the treasures of wisdom and knowledge of the universe (Colossians 2:2–3). Human intelligence was given so we would benefit from the technology that scientific research gives us in all its potential and capabilities for the good of mankind.

When we look at the intelligence of the created order it is there so we can know, believe, and relate intelligently to the God of purpose and design. It is not there so we can conclude that the wonder of the world we live in was all one big accident with no intelligent purpose or meaning. With God no longer at the center of meaning and purpose, humanity looks to the material world to give life meaning.

The Material World as God

Once we start to believe God is not real the focus in life becomes a materialistic one. Humanity moves from the supernatural to the natural. Mankind begins to put his trust in creation rather than in the Creator. He begins to build his life only on the comfort and security the material world can give Paul said:

> Who exchanged the truth of God for the lie, and wor-
> shiped and served the creature rather than the Creator,
> who is blessed forever. Amen.   Romans 1:25

Pleasure Becomes Life's Ultimate Purpose

Without God as the true meaning and purpose for life and with materialism unable to provide any real answers to life's big questions, humanity has no place to land except to live for all the pleasure we can get out of life. The popular slogan of the self-made man is "you only live once, so live it up." Unfortunately, the life given to pleasure comes with an expiration date.

> For this reason God gave them up to vile passions...
>   Romans 1:26

Pleasure Turns to Violence

When the parameters of life become blurred and with an expiration date on a life given to pleasure, life in the fast lane ultimately crashes into complete chaos. Pleasure without meaning and purpose rooted in God ultimately turns to violence, with everyone doing what they believe is right in their own eyes. Self-worship is the greatest threat to the common good of humanity, Paul said:

> And even as they did not like to retain God in their knowledge, God gave them over to a debased mind, to do those things which are not fitting... Romans 1:28

From a big-picture perspective, life's most important factor comes down to what Chip Ingram says in his book *God: As He Longs for You to See Him*: "What you think about God shapes your whole relationship with him. In addition, what you believe God thinks about you determines how close you will grow toward him."[1] Life never grows or advances beyond our concept of God, and people ultimately build their lives around what they think is true and right.

Chapter 2

What Atheists, Agnostics, and Christians All Have in Common

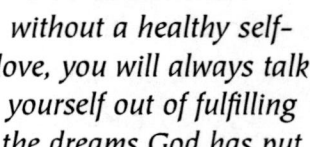

All People Need Love

A ll people need love, acceptance and belief in their personal worth. Nothing good, significant, or rewarding can ever be attempted by people who don't have healthy self-love. In fact, without healthy self-love you will always talk yourself out of fulfilling the

without a healthy self-love, you will always talk yourself out of fulfilling the dreams God has put in your heart

dreams God has put in your heart. Acceptance is what creates our sense of worth and value, as such, it is the basic ingredient of life. Within acceptance there is an empowerment that propels humans to the task of living life with the expectancy of thriving and succeeding. Acceptance energizes our creativity, often it manifests itself in goodwill towards others while at the same time creating personal satisfaction. Acceptance is what makes us feel safe amidst life's challenges and disappointments and what allows us to believe again when challenged by difficult life circumstances.

Without Acceptance the Human Spirit Withdraws and Dies

In the conversation Jesus initiated with the Samaritan woman, we immediately see the withdrawal of a heart who felt the disapproval of other human beings. From the very beginning, it is apparent that the Samaritan woman had no inclination to grant what would have taken minimal effort on her part. After all, how much physical effort would she have had to exert in order to give one cup of water to a thirsty traveler? How much time in her busy schedule would be lost for taking a few moments to grant this simple request?

The most humane response for most of us would have been to give the cup of water and be on our way, but not in this case. Why? When the Samaritan woman saw that the one asking for a drink of water was of Jewish descent, all she could think of was not how easy a common courtesy could have brightened the day for both the giver and receiver; instead, the only thing she could focus on was the fact that Jewish people considered Samaritans second-class citizens.

> Then the woman of Samaria said to Him, "How is it that You, being a Jew, ask a drink from me, a Samaritan woman?" *For the Jews have no dealings with Samaritans*. John 4:9, emphasis added

The thought of doing something so minimal for someone who in her mind claimed race superiority was the driving force behind her thoughts, feelings, and ultimately her actions. While the Savior's request for a drink of water was real, He takes this opportunity to lead this woman into the higher issues of life by giving her the acceptance she had refused to give Him.

> Jesus answered and said to her, "If you knew the gift
> of God, and who it is who says to you, 'Give Me a
> drink,' you would have asked Him, and He would
> have given you living water."   John 4:10

Notice that before Jesus revealed the complicated side of her life, He had already demonstrated unconditional love and acceptance by assuring her that the gift of God was greater than what she had, and that the giver of that gift was present and more willing to give her living water than she was willing to give Him physical water. The initial acceptance given to her begins to break down her inability to accept and reciprocate kindness. As more light begins to flood her heart, the attitude previously displayed from a heart filled with a history of rejection begins to soften. In the end she leaves her water pot. Acceptance is what everybody needs, and when it is missing in our lives it complicates the way we live with self and with others. In the absence of acceptance and approval there is a disorientation in life that usually doesn't fit reality. This condition ultimately leads to personal withdrawal where many of our basic social needs go unmet.

As in the case with the Samaritan woman, people have the tendency to become reckless with their lives and turn evil toward themselves and towards others when their need for love and approval are denied. Acceptance is critical to life's well-being. Call it whatever you want—'self-worth,' 'self-esteem,' or something else—the truth however cannot be denied; acceptance is what determines how well you get along with self and how well you get along with others. Human creativity flourishes when we feel genuinely loved and accepted. God's love and approval through Jesus Christ is what creates our greatest sense of worth and value which in turn allows us to believe and see value in others.

This is precisely what happens in justification. God accepts sinners as His very own sons and daughters through the sacrificial death of His Son Jesus Christ. The cross is the greatest demonstration of God's love toward sinners and the basis for believing that our lives have great eternal value in His eyes.

God's love and approval through Jesus Christ is what creates our greatest sense of worth and value which in turn allows us to believe and see value in others.

What then shall we say to these things? If God is for us, who can be against us? He who did not spare His own Son, but delivered Him up for us all, how shall He not with Him also freely give us all things?

Romans 8:31–32

Our creativity flourishes and our confidence to expect positive outcomes in life grows under God's acceptance and approval in spite of the fact that we still live in a fallen world. He promises to bring good things out of all our experiences in life, even the bad stuff we all go through.

We are confident that God is able to orchestrate every-thing to work toward something good and beautiful when we love Him and accept His invitation to live according to His plan.   Romans 8:28 VOICE

All People Need Character Growth

Second, atheists, agnostics, and Christians all need growing up. John Henry Newman said, "Growth is the only evidence of life." Nature confirms this truth; everything under God's control grows and serves an intelligent purpose in life. Trees grow and give their shade in the summer and provide homes for many species of life. The grass grows and provides food for many of God's creatures, in addition to making possible the plush golf courses men and women enjoy playing on. Flowers bloom and give their beauty and fragrance to amaze our sense of sight and smell.

While both nature and human physical growth share God's programming that allows for automatic growth, there is an aspect to human growth that must be learned and nurtured. Character is the human side of growth that is not automatic, it must be learned and nurtured. Character growth is the most important growth that can accompany natural human giftedness. Without character growth the endless possibilities

Without character growth, the endless possibilities of where your God-given giftedness and potential can lead will be short-lived. Success in life is always talent plus character

of where your God given talent and potential can lead to will be short-lived. Success in life is always talent plus character that always proves to be the winning hand in life.

> For "He who would love life and see good days, Let him refrain his tongue from evil, And his lips from speaking deceit. Let him turn away from evil and do good; Let him seek peace and pursue it. For the eyes of the LORD *are* on the righteous, And His ears *are open* to their prayers; But the face of the LORD *is* against those who do evil." 1 Peter 3:10-12

Some of the world's most gifted and talented people have had short-lived success not because they ran out of talent, but because they didn't have the character to support their talent and giftedness. Success in life is always about growing into the best version you can be of yourself. This is precisely what happens in sanctification. Through the Holy Spirit, God begins His extreme character makeover in your life. The nine characteristics of the fruit of the Holy Spirit mentioned in Galatians 5 are God's very own character being formed in your life. His character in you is what makes you both beautiful and strong throughout the duration of life. Without godly character, life has a tendency to give into the darkness that surrounds us and that leads us to finish life with regret and shame.

All People Need Purpose

Third, atheists, agnostics, and Christians need purpose in life. If you were asked what would allow you to experience the greatest fulfillment in life? Your automatic response might be money—lots more money. There is no doubt that more money usually means an increase in your material lifestyle—perhaps a more expensive house, a more expensive car, more expensive clothes, more expensive food, or just more expensive stuff.

Everything changes when money grows. However, if your pursuit of life fulfillment is based on the ability to acquire more material things, this probably indicates that your definition of personal life fulfillment is defined by comfort living. Although there is nothing inherently evil in material things, if there is a weak side to comfort living based on material things, it is in the fact that the thrill of it is short-lived. We all know from personal life experience that our material things sooner or later end up in the garage collecting dust, or as a garage sale item, or perhaps as a Goodwill tax deduction.

If you always need more or the advanced version of the same things you already have, then obviously these things are not leading to a sustained fulfillment in life, but only to an endless pursuit of a fulfillment that continues to elude you. This was probably at the heart of Solomon's disillusionment with life when he wrote:

If you always need more or the advanced version of the same things you already have, then obviously these things are not leading to a sustained fulfillment in life

> So I became great and excelled more than all who were before me in Jerusalem. Also my wisdom remained with me. Whatever my eyes desired I did not keep from them. I did not withhold my heart from any pleasure, for my heart rejoiced in all my labor; and this was my reward from all my labor. Then I looked on all the works that my hands had done and on the labor in which I had toiled; and indeed all was vanity and grasping for the wind. There was no profit under the sun. Ecclesiastes 2:9–11

True fulfillment in life is not in material comfort but in spiritual purpose. This is the call and adventure of redemption. Every born again child of God becomes an extension of God's kingdom purpose to encourage, and inspire others through his or her own

True fulfillment in life is not in material comfort, but in spiritual purpose.

God-story. In the life of the redeemed, everyone has a God-story to tell and a mission to embark on. What is equally important to understand is that our kingdom assignment is the key to our fulfillment in life.

A great misconception in our culture is the belief that quantity makes quality. This is not true; what makes quality in life is spiritual calling. A second great misconception is that spiritual calling is only for pastors, evangelists, missionaries, deacons, or elders. This misconception causes many in the body of Christ to disregard what is the most important factor in their life fulfillment. Justification and sanctification are great Christian truths, but these truths are not what lead to life fulfillment. More accurately, justification and sanctification are what prepare you for your kingdom purpose. It is your kingdom purpose that leads to your life fulfillment.

Unfortunately, as we have already noted, many of God's people have limited redemption to the forgiveness of sin and the assurance of heaven, but with no real substance in between. In this particular way of seeing redemption, being a Christian is nothing more than God forgiving you; punching your ticket to heaven, and then just waiting the rest of your life for your departing trip home. There isn't anything more boring and mentally agonizing to the creativity of human beings created in the image of God to accomplish nothing. You were not created to do nothing; you were not even created for things, you were created for purpose — His purpose. Without your God adventure, Christian life defaults to pursuing the same things the world pursues for life fulfillment.

> Do not love the world or the things in the world. If anyone loves the world, the love of the Father is not in him. For all that *is* in the world — the lust of the flesh, the lust of the eyes, and the pride of life — is not of the Father but is of the world. And the world is passing away, and the lust of it; but he who does the will of God abides forever. 1 John 2:15-17

All People Need Hope

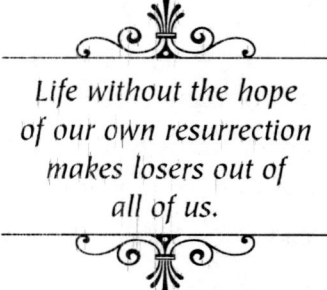

Fourth, atheists, agnostics, and Christians need hope that transcends their own lives. God's answer to the ultimate disappointment in life is the glorification that is in the gospel of Jesus Christ. Glorification is what awaits every Christian, and as such, it is the end of the experience of life in a fallen world and

Life without the hope of our own resurrection makes losers out of all of us.

the beginning of a glorious eternity with God. Life without the hope of our own resurrection makes losers out of all of us.

It doesn't matter how significant your life may have been, how fulfilling it may have been, or how many others were inspired through your contribution to life; in the end we all just die. In all honesty, nobody is okay with just dying. The truth is we all want to prolong life and fear death because there is a certain mystery about it. In fact, in 1 Corinthians 15, the Bible calls death "our enemy," and rightly so.

Nothing in human experience is more wretched than death and dying. Perhaps it's because we humans always seek security through what we control, and death is something we cannot control (1 Corinthians 15:26). Nevertheless, Paul wrote to Timothy, saying that Jesus Christ was revealed to put death to death and bring life and immortality (2 Timothy 1:10). The greatest truth and comfort of the gospel is not that it brings the greatest acceptance in life, nor is it that it brings the greatest transformation in life. It is not even that it brings the greatest adventure in life. The greatest truth and comfort of the gospel of Jesus Christ is that we never really die. Instead, death is the passing from the reality of a fallen world to the reality of God's world John writes:

Now I saw a new heaven and a new earth, for the first heaven and the first earth had passed away. Also there was no more sea. Then I, John, saw the holy city, New Jerusalem, coming down out of heaven from God, prepared as a bride adorned for her husband. And I heard a loud voice from heaven saying, "Behold, the tabernacle of God is with men, and He will dwell with them, and they shall be His people. God Himself will be with them and be their God. And God will wipe away every tear from their eyes; there shall be no more death, nor sorrow, nor crying. There shall be no more pain, for the former things have passed away." Then He who sat on the throne said, "Behold, I make all things new." And He said to me, "Write, for these words are true and faithful."   Revelation 21:1–5

Through the promise of victory over death Paul affirmed that life is worth living, but more importantly, in the end, life will be worth dying too.

For to me, to live is Christ and to die is gain.

Philippians 1:21

"O Death, where is your sting? O Hades, where is your victory?" The sting of death is sin, and the strength of sin is the law. But thanks be to God, who gives us the victory through our Lord Jesus Christ. Therefore, my beloved brethren, be steadfast, immovable, always abounding in the work of the Lord, knowing that your labor is not in vain in the Lord.

1 Corinthians 15:55–58

Chapter 3

Getting Past Empty Religion

As a child growing up in a family who had roots in both Protestantism and Catholicism, I often attended both services, depending on whose side of the family I was forced to go to church with. Protestant churches always scared me and made me feel that God was angry with me for being a sinner. While the pastor may have had the good intention of scaring me into a relationship with God through his fire and brimstone sermons, more often the only thing that really occurred was my being scared out of a relationship with God. Attending the Catholic church with my mother never scared me, but I was always thankful to God when the Mass was over.

From my childhood experiences; my idea of God was simple, God was always angry, and God was always boring. At least, this was the image that was being communicated to me about God and the very thing that drove me further away from God. Obviously when we lose sight of God's original intent, life is thrown into compete chaos as we try to reinvent it with very little success.

Myles Monroe said it best in his book *Understanding the Purpose and Power of Men:* "Where purpose is not known, abuse is inevitable."[2] I understand my confession may be difficult to hear. Be assured, my intention is not to demean anyone's religious background; I am simply retelling my experience growing up under the influence of authoritarian religion. How could I commit my life to a God who was always angry at me and always boring? I know not all church attendees can relate to my experience, and that in itself is a very good thing. Maybe you were one of the fortunate ones who grew up in a healthy church body where the focus of preaching and teaching was to empower life, not to condemn life. I guess I just happened to be one of the unluckiest church thumpers of the world, the Charlie Brown of church attendees.

Perhaps you should not be too upset with my confession. Perhaps the greater anger and agitation to those reading should be towards the fact that I went through this experience, and that through it, my concept of God was anything but crystal clear. Perhaps the greater alarm should be towards the fact that today many church attendees—hopefully, not the ones attending your church—are seeking help for their everyday problems outside of what is being preached and taught in the church. This should really stir up church people because when this happens, it implies God's truth is irrelevant to real life issues.

The Limits of Fear Theology

In the community of faith, the desire to encourage people towards a relationship with God is supreme; it is our highest calling, right under the worship of God. God wants to be known. However, using fear to motivate people to turn to God is short-lived, and in the end, fails to produce meaningful change and true relationship with God.

This is mainly because in fear theology, the main goal is to avoid consequences rather than to grow in an intimate understanding of who God is and to grasp the reality that the all-knowing; all-powerful, all-merciful God who rules the universe, is also our heavenly Father through the redemption that is in Jesus Christ.

in fear theology, the main goal is to avoid consequences rather than to grow in understanding that the all-knowing, all-powerful, all-merciful God who rules the universe is also our heavenly Father through the redemption that is in Jesus Christ.

Fear is still by far the weaker motivation in bringing out the best in people. I can easily compel my son to clean his room simply by assuring him that if he doesn't, there will be harsh consequences. The boy being smart enough to weigh the situation and not wanting to be grounded for the weekend, will easily comply with Dad's wishes, not because he values a clean room, but because he wants to avoid consequences that don't fit his weekend schedule. As a father, I may conclude that I have taught my son the value of cleanliness.

Later in life when I visit him in his own home and see that he lives in a messy house, I will awaken to the fact that I never really influenced his life for the good, as I had thought. All I really did was use fear to motivate his actions. That's the way fear motivation works. It's good only until the fear factor is removed. When it is removed by my son's moving away, the behavior of cleaning his room is no longer valid because it was never his to begin with.

Often—not always, but more often than we want to admit—children raised in church attending families grow up to be non-church attendees as adults. Why does this happen? It was never theirs to begin with. They attended church; but church never attended them, they just passed through church, but the message of the truth never passed through them. They were motivated to attend out of the fear of consequences. Over the years I've realized that the biggest problem with fear theology is that it doesn't require intelligent examination. The only thing you have to know and remember is to fear God. That becomes the catch-all answer. Don't do this or that because God will punish you. If there were a Christian slogan today, it would be the opposite of the "no fear" Nike commercials. In authoritarian religion, the slogan is always "more fear."

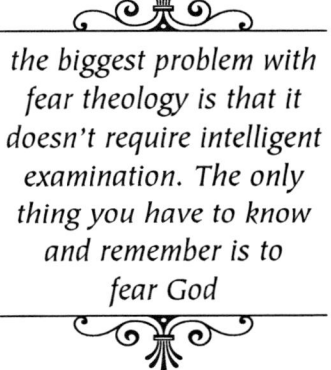

the biggest problem with fear theology is that it doesn't require intelligent examination. The only thing you have to know and remember is to fear God

It should be noted that the greatest commandment given to the followers of Jesus Christ was not to fear more, but to love more. Jesus said that there was no greater commandment than to love God with all your heart, soul, mind, and strength (Mark 12:30). I will confess that in my infancy in Christendom, I often wondered why God demanded so much attention from created beings who were basically nonessential to His glory. Later I realized that if man is to reach his potential in life, he must be a constant student of God because he was created in His image.

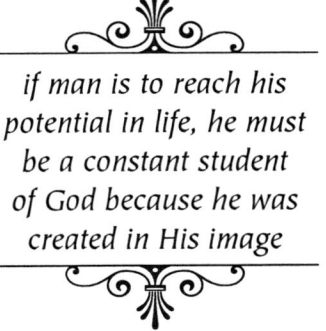

if man is to reach his potential in life, he must be a constant student of God because he was created in His image

It is important what you pursue with all your heart, soul, mind, and strength, because you become it. When Jesus laid out this grand commandment, He was actually identifying how we can come out of our own personal darkness and into the greatest potential of our lives. In the seventies, I remember a very popular bumper sticker; I actually had one myself. It read, "God said it, I believe it, and that settles it." While it conveyed the idea of loyalty and unwavering commitment to God which I consider to be the supreme duty of man, it might be beneficial to know why God says the things He says. The result of fear theology is that it has created a generation of Christians who can't explain their own beliefs, nor can they explain why their beliefs work in real-life situations.

The incredible generation of shrinking Christians has resulted in the need to have both a pastor and a therapist at our side; the pastor to explain how you should behave in church and the therapist to explain how life really works. Please don't misunderstand me; I am not against Christian counseling, being a counselor myself. The issue that I have with this practice is that it suggests the gospel is insufficient and inadequate to help us deal with the everyday stresses of life and our growth needs.

Obviously the next step down in this progression is to question whether we really need the words of the preacher. What good are the words of the preacher if it's my therapist who is giving me the options and solutions to life's problems and challenges?

The Limits of Ritualistic Theology

While fear theology seeks to scare us into a relationship with God, ritualistic theology seeks to substitute God with rituals. In other words, you get God through the rituals. As long as you practice the rituals, you are safe. Although a life devoted to practicing rituals can make you a very religious person, seldom does it change your heart which is the heart of the matter. Consider the ministry of the Pharisees to whom Jesus gave His harshest criticism. They were extremely religious in behavior, but as the representatives of the God who is love and mercy, their religiosity always proved to be inadequate in the context of what hurting people needed from them.

Instead of reflecting the love, mercy, and the empowerment of God, they often appeared legalistic, critical, and with a sense of superiority over others. Rituals mean absolutely nothing if you are not growing in Christ-likeness. Perhaps that was one of the points Jesus was making in the parable of the two men who prayed. You can be religious and still not be in true relationship with God.

> Also He spoke this parable to some who trusted in themselves that they were righteous and who despised others: Two men went up to the temple to pray, one a Pharisee and the other a tax collector. The Pharisee stood and prayed thus with himself, "God, I thank You that I am not like other men—extortioners, unjust, adulterers, or even as this tax collector. I fast twice a week; I give tithes of all that I possess." And the tax collector, standing afar off, would not so much as raise his eyes to heaven, but beat his breast, saying, "God, be merciful to me a sinner!" I tell you, this man went down to his house justified rather than the other; for everyone who exalts himself will be humbled, and he who humbles himself will be exalted. Luke 18:9–14

That's the problem with a religious system that is void of a relationship with God. Seldom does it lead to change that reflects Christ-like love the ultimate end of Christian life and ministry. Rituals were never intended to give us God. Perhaps their purpose was to reflect certain aspects of God. Unfortunately, in some instances they have replaced God, which has resulted in religious performances that are empty of God's presence and power. In contrast to fear theology where people just get exhausted from never doing enough to please God, a religious system that offers only ritualistic performances ultimately becomes irrelevant to life, especially to the younger generation who seek a God who is alive and relevant to real-life issues.

While many wise adults have been able to get past the intimidation of fear theology and the emptiness of ritualism to live productive Christian lives; for many others, fear theology and ritualistic religion are what turns them off from knowing the God of the Bible and from experiencing the abundant life Jesus promised. The focus in highlighting my concern with fear religion is not to paint a picture of a soft God who is all love and no discipline. There is always a healthy place for a father's correction, especially if it's the heavenly Father's correction. The Bible says God corrects those he loves (Proverb 3:12).

There are plenty of examples in the Old Testament where it was necessary for God to take His people, and sometimes even His servants to the woodshed. However, even in times of hard discipline, God never acted from a vindictive purpose as an end in itself. In the Old Testament, God's discipline was always for the purpose of reconciliation and restoration. In no particular way am

We don't need a soft gospel, nor do we need a hard gospel. What we really need is an empowering gospel, the gospel Jesus and Paul preached.

I advocating for a soft gospel. We don't need a soft gospel, nor do we need a hard gospel, what we really need is an empowering gospel, the gospel Jesus and Paul preached.

> For I am not ashamed of the gospel of Christ, for it
> is the power of God to salvation for everyone who
> believes, for the Jew first and also for the Greek.
>
> Romans 1:16

Church sinners, those who attend church on a regular basis would not deny the universality of sin. The reason we attend church in the first place is that we want to live victoriously, especially over self-destructive behavior. Unfortunately, the familiar message we get in fear theology is not one that empowers, but one that leaves us discouraged about our Christianity.

Preachers and teachers of the New Testament covenant of grace in Jesus Christ need to be reminded that the gospel, at its very core, is about life empowerment, not faultfinding. Jesus told Peter to feed His lambs and His sheep, not to beat them down. Notice the process of growth. Through proper care and feeding lambs can grow up to become strong healthy sheep (John 20:15–17). We all know we're sinners. The consequence of sin—death—is difficult to deny, even for atheists (Romans 6:23). What we need from the teaching ministry of the church is the knowledge of how the gospel of power translates into my everyday victory in life. Unfortunately, some clergy still prefer to crack the whip on Sunday mornings and drive their congregations like cattle instead of leading them like sheep. If we continue to remain indifferent towards a biblical curriculum that meets the needs of where people live, the message we are indirectly communicating to a generation searching for meaning and purpose is that the God of the Bible and His message are irrelevant to real-life issues.

Find What You Were Looking For?

It seems that in today's world everyone is pursuing better things in life. I don't believe this reflects an attitude that is biblically unworthy. After all, Jesus Himself said that He came to give life and to give it more abundantly (John 10:10). Perhaps the desire for better comes from feeling stuck in life or feeling like life is always in reverse gear. Even worse, maybe we do find what we were looking for only to be greatly disappointed. Even Solomon with all his wealth and things to do felt a deep emptiness from being disconnected from life's true purpose.

> Whatever my eyes desired I did not keep from them. I did not withhold my heart from any pleasure, for my heart rejoiced in all my labor; and this was my reward from all my labor. Then I looked on all the works that my hands had done and on the labor in which I had toiled; and indeed all was vanity and grasping for the wind. There was no profit under the sun.
>
> Ecclesiastes 2:10–11

How true it is that nothing in this world after experiencing it for the first time, can keep on fascinating us like it did the first time, and the quality of things fade into nothing in the routine of daily life. Perhaps the worst-case scenario is getting comfortable with just surviving. We feel like something important is still missing from life but it doesn't really matter because we have adjusted well to mediocrity.

Perhaps the greatest problem we all suffer from is having lost the fundamental truths that keep life moving in a forward direction. Maybe we have forgotten that the greatest forward mover in life is God Himself. A review of some of the encounters Jesus had with people should leave no doubt that God desires for us to move forward in life and not remain stuck.

- To the Samaritan woman, Jesus offered living water that would quench her thirst (John 4).

- To the weary and heavy burdened, Jesus offered rest and an easy yoke (Matthew 11).

- To the adulteress, Jesus offered forgiveness and a new beginning (John 8).

- To ordinary fishermen, Jesus offered to make them world-changers (Matthew 4).

- To the poor in spirit, Jesus offered them the kingdom of heaven (Matthew 5).

- To those obsessed with material things, Jesus offered treasure that would never rust, that thieves could never steal, and that insects could not destroy (Matthew 6).

- To those in spiritual captivity, Jesus offered freedom (Mark 5).

- To those who doubted, Jesus gave conclusive revelation (John 20).

- To those with unsettled minds, Jesus gave reassurance (Matthew 1).

- To those who accepted His calling, Jesus equipped with His power to minister effectively (Luke 9).

Perhaps the reason the life we all want to experience continues to elude us is that when we start planning for a great life, we start at the wrong place. Usually our life planning begins with identifying our personal preferences. Although there is nothing wrong with our preferences, the most fundamental question in life is not about money, people, things, or stuff.

Life's ultimate question comes down to essence; who are you at the core of your being? Answering this question is by far the better place to begin sorting out what matters most in life. The reason for this is that you cannot live in contradiction to your true self and yet continue to live well consistently. When you answer the question of who you are, the path in life becomes clearer and the obstacles that hinder your God-given destiny are easily weeded out. The promise of God is that when you truly begin to live from your true self, instead of from the outside in everything else in life that matters falls into its proper place.

> But seek first the kingdom of God and His righteous-
> ness, and all these things shall be added to you.
>
> Matthew 6:33

Life fulfillment comes from living out of what God has built inside of you. Don't try to be someone else, live who you are. Robert Jeffress says in *Guilt Free Living*: "Some people have jobs they don't like in order to buy things they don't need to impress the people they don't like."[3]

So then who are you at the core of your being? Here's the truth about the most important question of life and the key to rediscovering life's true purpose and fulfillment, you were created in the image of God. In his book *Following Christ*, Joseph M. Stowell says: "Being created in God's image means we are designed for a reflective following relationship with our Creator. Adam and Eve were given responsibilities that defined how they were to follow and then were released to enjoy all he had made. God was the singular pursuit of their lives, and their environment was a place to express their followership as an act of gratitude and love."[4] God's redemption is all about restoring your relationship with Him. He and He alone is the source of your meaning, your purpose, your hope and fulfillment in life. For this very reason every Christian should master the meaning of redemption, and everyone who is still searching for that elusive better should carefully reexamine what the gospel of Jesus Christ brings to the whole human experience.

Chapter 4

Life's Greatest Acceptance
(How God Accepts Us)

G od's love and desire to step into broken humanity; redeem us from our fallen condition, and restore us to the place of blessing and favor, will forever be the greatest comeback known throughout the history of mankind. God's plan to restore our lives involves a four-part process known as *redemption*, or *salvation*. Both of these words in Scripture communicate the same idea, while the parts of redemption often appear to stand alone throughout the New Testament. The fact that redemption unfolds as an interconnecting process in the life of a believer is brought into focus no more clearly than in Paul's letter to the Romans.

> For whom He foreknew, He also predestined to be *conformed* to the image of His Son, that He might be the firstborn among many brethren. Moreover whom He predestined, these He also *called*; whom He called, these He also *justified*; and whom He justified, these He also *glorified*.
>
> Romans 8:29–30, emphasis added

As Paul revealed this great truth, he was not so much concerned with giving us the order in which redemption happens. Paul's main concern was in showing us how all these four parts of redemption are intricately connected to each other. In other words, it is not possible to just get one piece of redemption without the others. All the parts of redemption connect to reflect one single truth—redemption! The following illustration perhaps will help us envision the process as one whole.

Romans 8:29–30

Justification	**Acceptance**	Right standing
Sanctification	**Growth**	Right living
Calling	**Fulfillment**	Right purpose
Glorification	**Hope**	Right ending

In the first part of redemption as we can see from this illustrative chart, the concern is with how God accepts sinners as His very own sons and daughters. For acceptance to have a sustained positive influence on how humans change and grow, God's acceptance must come with a "no return" policy. In other words, once God has accepted us, our acceptance cannot be lost or revoked; otherwise the positive influence that acceptance can have on our lives will only last up until our first major meltdown. No one can survive

No one can survive with an acceptance policy that allows for only one mistake. None of us can live that well; only Jesus lived consistently perfect and holy.

with an acceptance policy that allows for only one mistake. None of us can live that well, only Jesus lived consistently perfect and holy. In God's acceptance we are not the ones who are holding on to God, instead, God is holding on to us.

> And I give them eternal life, and they shall never perish; neither shall anyone snatch them out of My hand. My Father, who has given them to Me, is greater than all; and no one is able to snatch them out of My Father's hand.   John 10:28-29

How Can We Know God Has Accepted Us?

For the community of faith, the ultimate acceptance that makes everything else in life move forward begins with God. The basic assumption in the community of faith is that redemption begins with God's plan for accepting us as His very own sons and daughters. Biblical redemption is God acting through the person of Jesus Christ for the purpose of redeeming fallen man.

Through Christ, sinners who would be eternally lost stand before God in complete, undeniable acceptance as His own sons and daughters. At Calvary this was the main concern being addressed. For this reason, the cross of Jesus Christ will forever stand as the final determining factor regarding man's fate on earth and his eternal destiny.

God's Plan for Accepting Us

> Knowing that a man is not justified by the works of the law but by faith in Jesus Christ, even we have believed in Christ Jesus, that we might be justified by

faith in Christ and not by the works of the law; for by the works of the law no flesh shall be justified.

Galatians 2:16

To understand how great God's redemption is towards sinners, we need to consider the holiness of God in contrast to the sinfulness of man. When we speak of holiness in reference to God two things stand out. First, by the holiness of God it is understood that He is separate and different from us. He is self-existent, self-determined, and eternal. We, on the other hand are created beings dependent on things we cannot control, and are always physically diminishing, that's our nature. Second, by the holiness of God, it is also understood that He is different from us in terms of character. This is probably the most common way we think about God. He is eternally pure, perfect, and without sin. We, on the other hand are fallen creatures who are not perfect and whose fallen nature is the very opposite of God's holiness. Paul describes our own fallen nature in contrast to the holiness of God.

> As it is written:
> "There is none righteous, no, not one;
> There is none who understands;
> There is none who seeks after God.
> They have all turned aside;
> They have together become unprofitable;
> There is none who does good, no, not one."
> "Their throat is an open tomb;
> With their tongues they have practiced deceit";
> "The poison of asps is under their lips";
> "Whose mouth is full of cursing and bitterness."
> "Their feet are swift to shed blood;

Destruction and misery are in their ways;

And the way of peace they have not known."

"There is no fear of God before their eyes."

Romans 3:10–18

The holiness of God is what separates Him from all of His creation and from the other religious systems of the world. The fact that we were created in His image does not mean we share equality with Him. In many of the other religious systems of the world, acceptance with deity can be acquired through personal effort. Man is able, through his own merits, to work his way towards acceptance with his deity. If our idea of a creator is one whom we can appease with our very own religious works, then by definition he is probably not much higher than his worshipers. A god with whom human beings can negotiate and trade with is not by definition a god at all — perhaps just a stronger human being. The pharaohs of Egypt were considered gods even though they themselves could not resist or postpone the death and decay that come upon all men. A god you have to carry and put away in the closet for safe keeping after you worship him, is not a god by definition at all, only plaster created by man. The revelation of God's holiness in the Scripture is what makes Him far above and beyond all of His creation. There is absolutely nothing humans can do to negotiate their forgiveness and restoration for being in violation of His holy character.

God's Holiness Required Christ's Sacrifice

God's holiness was the very reason Jesus Christ needed to die on the cross. Without His death, the forgiveness of sin and acceptance with God would have been humanly impossible. Christ's death points to two realities. First, it points to the gravity of man's pitiful

54

condition, both his sin and his inability to redeem himself. Second, it points to the indescribable depths of God's holiness, something mankind has not yet fully understood and perhaps never will until we're home.

The reason Christ had to die on our behalf was because the sacrifice itself needed to be as holy as God Himself for it to have redeeming value. A sinner dying for sinners may earn someone a medal of honor, but it won't result in justification before the righteous, holy God. The sacrifice had to be His own Son, the perfect Lamb of God who takes away the sin of the world (John 1:29).

But if Jesus was God incarnate, how would it be possible for God to die on the cross? Christ needed to be both God and man in order to make redemption happen. If Christ had kept His full deity, death on the cross would have been impossible. On the other hand, if Christ had remained only a man and nothing else, His substitutionary death for mankind would have been of no redeeming value. On the cross of Calvary, Christ needed to be man in order to die and deity in order for His death to result in redemption. His life satisfied the righteous requirements of the law and His death satisfied the penalty for sin. His resurrection was proof that God accepted His sacrifice as the basis of our own acceptance with Him.

Christ, Our Substitution

In Scripture, the idea regarding the substitutionary death of Jesus Christ means that on the cross, God laid all the sin of mankind—past, present, and future—on Christ Himself. At Calvary, God took the wrath man deserved and placed it on His very own Son so that we wouldn't have to die the death of sin and face eternal separation from God.

As a result, the blood of Jesus has made us right with God now, and certainly we will be rescued by Him from God's wrath *in the future*. If we were in the heat of combat with God when His Son reconciled us by laying down His life, then how much more will we be saved by Jesus' *resurrection* life?

Romans 5:9–10 VOICE

Righteousness in the Bible

For He made Him who knew no sin to be sin for us, that we might become the righteousness of God in Him. 2 Corinthians 5:21

In the Bible, the word *righteousness* appears often throughout both the Old and New Testaments. Depending on the context, the word *righteousness* can have different meanings. The most common interpretation of this word is to see it as a reference to moral conduct. However, righteousness in the Bible is not always associated with moral character. Sometimes it is a reference to imputed or gifted righteousness. There is a big difference between the righteousness that is acquired of man through law keeping and the righteousness that is imputed or gifted to man. To understand the difference between the two uses and how righteousness plays a significant role in our own acceptance with God, consider the following scriptures regarding righteousness in both the Old and New Testaments.

Various Uses of Righteousness in the Bible

"For I say to you, that unless your **righteousness** exceeds the righteousness of the scribes and Pharisees, you will by no means enter the kingdom of heaven."

Matthew 5:20

"But we are all like an unclean thing, and all our **righteousnesses** are like filthy rags; we all fade as a leaf, and our iniquities, like the wind, have taken us away."

Isaiah 64:6

"For He made Him who knew no sin to be sin for us, that we might become the **righteousness** of God in Him."

2 Corinthians 5:21

Righteousness to Stand On

All of these verses use the word *righteousness* with extreme implications. In Matthew, Jesus makes righteousness mandatory for entering the kingdom of heaven. The reference to the righteousness of the scribes and Pharisees sets the standard high, since those who considered themselves to be righteous were far from the righteousness required by God. Additionally, the verse points to the fact that no one will be in heaven by sheer accident or mistaken identity. This was probably the main point Christ was making in exposing the hypocrisy of the scribes and Pharisees. At the cost of publicly humiliating the scribes and Pharisees, perhaps the only hope we have to enter heaven is to try harder. The problem with a religious system of trying harder is in the next verse where the prophet Isaiah declares that all our righteousness are as filthy rags. If righteousness is an absolute for entering the kingdom of heaven, how are we to get in if we have no righteousness? Finally, there is the third verse where Paul says we have the righteousness of God through Christ.

How do we sort this out? One verse says we need righteousness to enter heaven, the next verse says we don't have the right kind of righteousness and the last verse says we have God's righteousness. Does the Bible contradict itself? Absolutely not. The key to understanding righteousness in relationship to how God accepts us is to distinguish between acceptance with God through earned righteousness and acceptance with God through gifted righteousness.

> For if by the one man's offense death reigned through
> the one, much more those who receive abundance of
> grace and of the *gift of righteousness* will reign in
> life through the One, Jesus Christ.
>
> Romans 5:17, emphasis added

Righteousness in the Old Testament

In the Old Testament covenant, righteous conduct was measured by strict adherence to God's perfect laws, laws that in reality were a reflection of God's own righteous character. Additionally, righteousness was necessary to be in right standing with God. Approval and acceptance with God were measured by how well one lived up to God's holy standards. To break one of God's holy commandments was to be in sin and in a state of unrighteousness which made a person unfit for God.

To compensate for the fact that no one could live up to God's standard of righteousness, animal sacrifices were instituted as sin offerings for the forgiveness of sin (unrighteous acts), but never as the means for permanent forgiveness of sin. For this reason, sin offerings through animal sacrifices were a repetitive observance.

This created a very complicated situation for people who were actively pursuing acceptance and approval with God for obvious reasons. One could offer a sin offering and be in right standing with God and one hour later be right back in need of forgiveness; out of right standing with God, and in need of another sin offering. Perhaps the greatest fear in this kind of religious system was the thought of actually dying before one could bring a sin offering and thus be in danger of eternal separation from God. This was how the religious system in the Old Testament operated, acceptance with God was measured by one's personal effort through law keeping.

Righteousness in the New Testament

In the New Testament, when the word *righteousness* is used together with the Lord Jesus Christ, it is not a reference to moral conduct as in the Old Testament. Rather, it is a righteousness that is gifted to man as in Romans 5:17. This gifted righteousness is imputed to us through Christ and becomes the basis of our own righteousness and acceptance with God.

> But now the *righteousness* of God apart from the law is revealed, being witnessed by the Law and the Prophets, even the righteousness of God, through faith in Jesus Christ, to all and on all who believe.
>
> Romans 3:21–22, emphasis added

In his letter written to the Philippians Paul said that the righteousness he clung to was not his own, but was the righteousness of God through faith in Jesus Christ.

Yet indeed I also count all things loss for the excel-
lence of the knowledge of Christ Jesus my Lord, for
whom I have suffered the loss of all things, and count
them as rubbish, that I may gain Christ and be found
in Him, not having my own righteousness, which is
from the law, but that which is through faith in Christ,
the righteousness which is from God by faith.

Philippians 3:8–9

Paul was not claiming any righteousness of his own, but depending
on Christ's righteousness as the means for his own right standing with
God. Additionally what is clear is that his righteousness in Christ was
not a reference to moral perfection, but only to righteous standing.
Paul himself admitted he had not yet reached perfection in a moral
sense, but he pressed on. However, with regard to his standing before
God, he had the righteousness of Christ.

Not that I have already attained, or am already per-
fected; but I press on, that I may lay hold of that for
which Christ Jesus has also laid hold of me.

Philippians 3:12

Justification Through Jesus Christ

Therefore we conclude that a
man is justified by faith apart
from the deeds of the law.

Romans 3:28

*justification is not a
reference to how one is
living or even how one
should live. The issue
in justification is strictly
about legal standing*

In the above passage the word *justified* means to be in right standing or
in righteous standing. It means that the

60

accusations and charges against man, those we saw back in Romans 3:10–18, have been forgiven and removed. It is extremely important to keep in mind that justification is not a reference to how one is living. The issue in justification is strictly about legal standing not moral conduct. Here is where many fall off the acceptance wagon, figuratively speaking. Obviously how we live is extremely important in God's redemptive purposes. However, in the process of redemption, justification is not the part where God begins to work through the Holy Spirit to change us. Justification is strictly dealing with the removal of our guilt before a holy righteous God. For this reason Paul says that there is no condemnation for those who are in Christ Jesus Romans 8:1. The process of change begins in sanctification. Keep in mind however, that when the process of sanctification begins, God has already accepted us as His son or daughter and declared us innocence and not guilty.

> But as many as received Him, to them He gave the right to become children of God, to those who believe in His name: who were born, not of blood, nor of the will of the flesh, nor of the will of man, but of God.
>
> John 1:12–13

The only thing that changes in justification is the way we should think about how we stand before God. Justification is not some probationary period in which, if we pass, God will make us one of His own. By the time we get to the sanctification part of redemption, we have already been eternally accepted. If you think acceptance with God is based on sanctification (*how you change*), biblically, you are living your redemption in reverse order, by putting sanctification ahead of justification. If you commit this error, what you are doing is making your performance the basis for how God accepts you instead of Christ's death and resurrection.

> Moreover, brethren, I declare to you the gospel which I preached to you, which also you received and in which you stand, by which also you are saved, if you hold fast that word which I preached to you — unless you believed in vain.   1 Corinthians 15:1-2

God will never accept you on the basis of how you change. He knows you can't change on your own. Rather, He changes you because He has already accepted you on the basis of the justification that is in Christ. The inward work of the Holy Spirit (sanctification) is the evidence that God has already accepted you for all eternity. Perhaps the difficulty in making this distinction is that justification and

God never accepts you on the basis of how you change. He changes you because He has already accepted you on the basis of the justification that is in Christ.

sanctification run parallel throughout redemption, with justification always first in the process. Without the *justification* and the imputed *righteousness* we have through Christ, no one can stand in peace and favor with God. We stand before Him only in our sin and thus deserving of condemnation.

That's the problem with the holiness of God in relation to man. No one can ever reach the point of acceptance with God through personal effort. The moment we try to add works to aid or influence how we stand before God, we no longer have New Testament salvation. God was completely working our acceptance with Him through Jesus Christ His Son. There is absolutely nothing men or women can do, nothing to their credit that will result in any kind of relational remedy with God. I think that is the point in John 1:12, where John says not by blood, nor the will of the flesh, nor the will of man, but only by God. God was working out our acceptance with Him through Christ alone without any aid from man.

Paul's Letter to the Galatians

Trying to make acceptance with God a fifty-fifty proposition where God does His part and we are left to fill in the blanks, is the very thing that initiated Paul's letter to the Galatians. Paul used very strong language in his letter to the Galatians as he sought to correct their error. Paul even went to the extreme of crediting their delusion to demonic influence.

> O foolish Galatians! Who has bewitched you that you should not obey the truth, before whose eyes Jesus Christ was clearly portrayed among you as crucified? This only I want to learn from you: Did you receive the Spirit by the works of the law, or by the hearing of Faith? Galatians 3:1-2

In contrasting *law keeping* with *grace keeping* as the means for *justification/acceptance*, Paul reminded them that if acceptance with God could be accomplished by individual effort through law keeping, there would have never been a need for Christ to die.

> I do not set aside the grace of God; for if righteousness [how we come to be accepted by God as his own] comes through the law [self-effort], then Christ died in vain Galatians 2:21, emphasis added

63

The fact that Christ died on our behalf indicates that man's ability to resolve the issue of acceptance and approval with God was beyond his means. Paul then appealed to what the Galatians had already experienced through the new grace covenant when he referred to the work of the Holy Spirit in them. Here the answer would be obvious, as they would be forced to acknowledge that they had not earned the gift of the Holy Spirit through the works of the law, but through faith in Christ.

> This only I want to learn from you: Did you receive
> the Spirit by the works of the law, or by the hearing
> of faith?   Galatians 3:2

Paul went on to say that those who seek acceptance with God through the works of the law are obligated to keep the whole law not just preferred parts of the law. If the law, through the inability of human weakness was the reason for man's guilt and condemnation, how could man return to his own efforts of law keeping as the basis for approval and acceptance with God?

> For as many as are of the works of the law are under
> the curse; for it is written, "Cursed is everyone who
> does not continue in all things which are written in
> the book of the law, to do them." But that no one is
> justified by the law in the sight of God is evident, for
> "the just shall live by faith."   Galatians 3:10–11

In his final argument, Paul said that the law was not given so that we could work out our own justification/acceptance with God. The law's purpose was to show us our guilt and lead us to the cross of Jesus Christ, where there is complete and absolute *acceptance* with our Creator.

> But before faith came, we were kept under guard by
> the law, kept for the faith which would afterward be
> revealed. Therefore the law was our tutor to bring us
> to Christ, that we might be justified by faith.
>
> Galatians 3:23–24

What Justification/Acceptance Means in the Spiritual Realm

(1) We Legally Belong to God

The accomplished work of Jesus Christ has given believers
legal standing with God. Paul wrote in Ephesians 2 about our legal
citizenship.

> Therefore remember that you, once Gentiles in the
> flesh—who are called Uncircumcision by what is
> called the Circumcision made in the flesh by hands—
> that at that time you were without Christ, being aliens
> from the commonwealth of Israel and strangers from
> the covenants of promise, having no hope and without
> God in the world. But now in Christ Jesus you who
> once were far off have been brought near by the blood
> of Christ; Now, therefore, you are no longer strangers
> and foreigners, but fellow citizens with the saints and
> members of the household of God.
>
> Ephesians 2:11–13, 19

This legal repositioning we have through Jesus Christ and not
through our own efforts has forever changed the way we stand before
God. We no longer stand alienated, separated and unknown to God.
Through Jesus Christ we legally and irrefutably belong to God.

(2) God Sees us in Christ's Righteousness

Through Christ, and not through human effort we have been given legal righteousness. Christ's righteousness has been imputed to us. This transfer of righteousness that has now been deposited into our human accounts has forever changed the way God sees us. God no longer sees us in the context of our sins and failures, but in the context of Christ's holiness and perfection, fully and completely pleasing to Him, fully and completely accepted and approved.

> And you, who once were alienated and enemies in your mind by wicked works, yet now He has reconciled in the body of His flesh through death, to present you holy, and blameless, and above reproach in His sight. Colossians 1:21–22

(3) Sin Doesn't Have the Last Word

Through Christ and His finished work on the cross we also have legal advocacy. No longer can sin defeat us and have the last word in our lives. Sin and its consequences have been forever defeated on the cross and by the advocacy of Christ Himself. How incredible and comforting to know that we stand before God fully accepted, fully approved, and fully loved in His sight through the accomplished work of Jesus Christ.

> My little children, these things I write to you, so that you may not sin. And if anyone sins, we have an Advocate with the Father, Jesus Christ the righteous. And He Himself is the propitiation for our sins, and not for ours only but also for the whole world. 1 John 2:1–2

What God's Justification/Acceptance Means in Everyday Life

The fact that we were created in the image of God all the more highlights the reason why our need for acceptance and reconciliation must first begin with God. From a biblical worldview, we understand that everyone born after Genesis 3 was born separated from God, our true source of security and significance. In this separation, every man and woman seeks someone or something on which to anchor life in order to give it a sense of value and completeness. Usually, in this approach it is not uncommon to try to anchor life on other people, a career, or material possessions. Most often it is in all of these or a combination of the three. Although there is nothing inherently wrong with these things, experience reminds us that the people we thought could be anchors for life often turn out to be anchors of disappointment and disillusionment. The difficulty in trying to find completeness in other people like ourselves lies in the fact that we all share a certain brokenness the Bible calls *sin*.

> For all have sinned and fall short of the glory of
> God.   Romans 3:23

Broken people plus other broken people never equal one whole; the only thing we really have is just two broken pieces. That is the problem with being human, we cannot find that "happily ever after" in other human beings who share the same selfish nature that is in all of us. I am not trying to scare anyone away from marriage. God created marriage to be the most significant relationship on earth and a healthy marriage is the foundation for a healthy society. Everyone wins when the marriage is good and everyone loses when the marriage breaks. The point, however is to acknowledge that being created in the image of God means that at the deepest level of our being, our true completeness can only be met through a reconnecting with God. The only thing broken people can do is to create more little broken people who grow up not knowing where to anchor life. Consider the great commandment given to us by Jesus Christ:

> "And you shall love the LORD your God with all your heart, with all your soul, with all your mind, and with all your strength." This is the first commandment. And the second, like it, is this: "You shall love your neighbor as yourself." There is no other command-ment greater than these.   Mark 12:30–31

Here the Lord Jesus points to a three-dimensional relationship that applies to every human being: God, self, and others. Loving God first is not about His ego. God has no such nature. Additionally, God doesn't need us in order for Him to be who He is. However, from the human side of life, we always need to begin with God as our reference point. This is because only through Him, can we know who we truly are with regards to our true identity.

The sequence in the Mark passage makes a lot of sense when you consider that the only way to be okay with loving others is to first know your own worth and significance in Christ. David G. Benner in *Surrender to Love* says: "Knowing ourselves to be deeply loved by God is the first step in becoming genuine great lovers of others and God."[5] Loving others as ourselves is not possible without first realizing how much God loves and values us.

Loving the people we are competing with to determine where we fit on the social ladder of success makes absolutely no sense at all. It doesn't matter whether we are competing in a beauty contest, spelling contest, talent contest, or spitting contest—it all feels like self-betrayal. In the relational equation of life God must always be first. It is only through Him that we see our true worth and value, or what I prefer to call our "God-esteem." A self created in God's image for God's glory and God's purpose, irrespective of how we measure up in comparison with the rest of the world. When our primary acceptance comes from God, we relinquish the need to have our worth and value determined by how others accept us or how we measure up with others.

Getting our acceptance and approval from God does not mean that we don't need life's other relationships. The one thing we can count on is that life is all about relationships. We were created to live in the context of relationships. However, what we don't need from our relationships is to be defined or destroyed by them. This is what usually happens in relationships that are only two-dimensional. When broken people seek validation from other broken people, the only thing that results is disappointment, anger, and resentment as we seek to obtain from others what they cannot give us. When our relationship with Christ is growing and lived out from the acceptance and validation He gives, we are better equipped to navigate successfully through life's other relationships. It allows us the freedom to forgive and not be controlled by life's insults that often lead to disappointment with ourselves and with others. It allows us the freedom not to be overcome by strongholds of anger, resentment, and other negative emotions that destroy us inwardly.

When broken people seek validation from other broken people, the only thing that results is disappointment, anger, and resentment as we seek to obtain from others what they cannot give us.

It should be noted that we will never be exempt from encounters with broken people. We all come into the world this way. However, what becomes different through a growing relationship with Christ is not that the world changes and becomes a better friendlier place. No, what happens is that we become a better version of ourselves through God's love and acceptance. The world then changes in response to our change. This doesn't mean that we will be immune to rejection and the difficult feelings rejection leaves. Rejection always feels ugly no matter who it comes from, even if it comes from a stranger. At the core of our being we were not created to be rejected but to be loved. The important thing to grasp in Christian spirituality is that our self-concept is either going to be built on God's love and acceptance or on people's love and acceptance.

As we have already noted, our ultimate self-worth cannot be built on other people who share the same brokenness that is in all of us. As such, God's acceptance will always give us the greatest opportunity to continue to grow and thrive in a world of broken people. His love and acceptance is our greatest springboard to experiencing the greatest sense of self-esteem and forward momentum in life.

However, if our vision of God's fatherhood is distorted, everything else that influences our self-esteem and forward momentum in life will be experienced from a distorted reality. Most frustrating will be the fact that no matter how hard we try, other people like ourselves cannot be the ultimate source of our completeness. The Samaritan woman noted earlier in the Gospel of John had failed through five marriages and was going on marriage number six (John 4:17–18).

Humans were never created to find their ultimate worth and meaning in other human beings. Adam and Eve were created to be life partners of God's amazing promises and recipients of a fulfillment in life that could only be realized through Him. With God as their true source of security and significance, they were able to live as life partners in complete harmony with each other, without the challenges of a broken world and the insecurities that strain relationships today.

The Tension Between Performance and Grace

The truth about how God accepts sinners as His very own sons and daughters is so incredibly beyond human thinking that it is hard to believe it is true. Perhaps influencing our disbelief is the fact that it flows in the opposite direction from how our minds have been programmed to think in a fallen world. Christians live between the conditioning acquired from the fallen world, in which acceptance and approval are always performance based, and the grace of God in which acceptance is never performance based, but faith based. The tension that exists between performance and grace is so strong that herein lies the mental conflict we so easily are overcome by. It is easier for all of us to revert to what we are most familiar with, in this case acceptance based on performance.

The reason we step back into performance-based acceptance with God and don't continue in the path of grace in accordance with John 1:16, is that after salvation, the world we wake up to every morning still operates on the principle of acceptance through performance. Naturally, what happens is that we bring this formula into our relationship with God. The results are that when we fail—and we all occasionally miss

> *The reason we step back into performance-based acceptance with God and don't continue in the path of grace in accordance with John 1:16 is that after salvation, the world we wake up to every morning still operates on the principle of acceptance through performance.*

the mark—we incorrectly assume that our acceptance with God is in jeopardy. The only possible outcome of a performance-based acceptance with God is frustration, guilt and shame. There can be no lasting peace and enduring joy in an acceptance with God that relies on human effort.

That's why Jesus Christ needed to come to earth. In living He fulfilled all the commandments of the law. In dying He paid the penalty for sin even though He was not guilty of committing any sin. His dying was the payment for sin on our behalf. His resurrection from the dead was God's way of accepting His atonement on our behalf. Through this we are eternally His to live life's greatest adventure—His adventure.

Chapter 5

Life's Greatest Exchange
(How God Grows Us)

For whom He foreknew, He also predestined to be
conformed to the image of His Son, that He might be
the firstborn among many brethren. Moreover whom
He predestined, these He also called; whom He called,
these He also justified; and whom He justified, these
He also glorified.   Romans 8:29–30

H aving lived with Jesus for approximately three years must have
been the most exciting time in the lives of the disciples. Think
about it for a moment. No other followers of world leaders would
have seen what the disciples of Jesus Christ saw. Imagine how many
miracles upon miracles they saw in those three short years, from
healing Peter's mother-in-law from a common fever to raising a wid-
ow's only son from the dead. It's no surprise why the disciples began
to feel a sense of entitlement. Realistically, who can blame them
even though we don't agree with their prideful attitude. It didn't
take very long for them to understand that nothing in the world they
lived in was greater than this Jesus who had called them to be His

life companions. Nature, sickness, disease, death, and the powers of darkness were all subject to the authority of Jesus with just one word. In fact, on one occasion the disciples' sense of entitlement went overboard, as they asked Jesus if He wanted them to command fire from heaven to destroy a village that had rejected them (Luke 9:54).

It should be of great comfort to know that with all the authority and power in His hands, His greatest power is love towards failing sinners. In chapter 14 of the Gospel of John, Jesus began to tell His disciples about His departure, something they did not fully understand until after His death and resurrection. He told them however, not to be troubled, He was going to prepare a place for them and would return when all things were ready. In the interim He promised not to leave them orphans. He was going to send them another one like Himself, referring to the Holy Spirit. He would continue to remain with them forever. Through the Holy Spirit, the presence of Jesus Christ who always protected them, nurtured them, met their needs, and empowered them would move from the outside to the inside. What would be the greater experience in life: Christ with us or Christ in us through the Holy Spirit?

This leads us to the second part of redemption where the concern now turns from acceptance to transformation, growth and maturity in life. Growing up and continuing life development is a very important part of life. In fact, growing up into the best you that you can be is the top priority behind all the self-help psychology. In God's redemptive purposes, your growth towards maturity in life is also a top priority. God is not only concerned with the forgiveness of your sin, He is also interested in your personal life development and your continued growth into maturity.

With no intention of sounding critical or demeaning, let me say that Christians at the beginning of their redemption are a saved mess. We have been adopted into the family of God and are His sons and daughters with all the privileges and blessings, nevertheless, we are still a big mess. It is important to understand that in sanctification we have been changed; we are being changed, and we will be changed. There is no need to become discouraged or disappointed in the process of growing into spiritual maturity. There is only the need to have complete trust in the redemption that is in Jesus Christ, the author and finisher of our faith and resist Satan's assault to make us feel unworthy and defeated. God's promise is to complete His good work in us.

> Being confident of this very thing, that He who has begun a good work in you will complete it until the day of Jesus Christ.   Philippians 1:6

The Holy Spirit: The Experience of Every Christian

The common belief among all New Testament believers is that the process of change and growth begins immediately at the point of faith in Jesus Christ. At that moment, the Holy Spirit of change and growth begins to occupy our lives. The apostle Paul said:

> In Him you also trusted, after you heard the word of truth, the gospel of your salvation; in whom also, having believed, you were sealed with the *Holy Spirit of promise*, who is the guarantee of our inheritance until the redemption of the purchased possession, to the praise of His glory.   Ephesians 1:13–14, emphasis added

In his book *Baptism and Fullness,* John Stott says: "Once He has taken up residence within us, making our body His temple, His work of sanctification begins. In brief, His ministry is both to reveal Christ to us and to form Christ in us, so that we grow steadily in our knowledge of Christ and in our likeness to Christ."[6] Through Him, we are empowered inwardly with the fruit and gifts of the Spirit to live and serve effectively in His kingdom purpose. In spite of this clarity in the Word of God, it is here that disagreement occurs in the body of Christ.

Some believe that the occupancy of the Holy Spirit is a two-phase filling that needs to be experienced by all believers. The way this plays out in Christian life is that the Holy Spirit of promise, the one Paul said we were seal with at the moment of faith, is seen as occupying the Christian in two stages. He occupies your life to some degree when you first trust in Jesus Christ as your Savior according to the Ephesians passage. However, it is possible for an even greater work of sanctification to occur when you receive a second filling, known as the "baptism of the Holy Spirit." The evidence that one has received this additional filling is by the ability to speak in tongues. In this case, the sealing of the Holy Spirit of promise and the baptism of the Holy Spirit of promise are really two separate promises.

The difficulty in a theology that embraces two promises of the Holy Spirit—one called the sealing of the Holy Spirit of promise, followed by a greater filling known as the of baptism of the Holy Spirit of promise—is that it is never acknowledged by any of the New Testament authors. Paul never commanded the believers at Ephesus to make sure they sought the baptism of the Holy Spirit of promise after having received the sealing of the Holy Spirit of promise. There is no scripture we can cite where the Lord Jesus Christ specifically said the Holy Spirit would be a two-stage process for future believers: a beginner's portion of the Holy Spirit of promise, known as the sealing, followed by a greater portion of the Holy Spirit, known as the baptism in the Holy Spirit of promise.

Peter never acknowledged a two-stage filling of the Holy Spirit. In his first sermon delivered at Pentecost, he simply preached faith in Jesus Christ, and said that on the basis of faith in Jesus, they too would receive the same gift that he and the other disciples had received.

> Then Peter said to them, "Repent, and let every one of you be baptized in the name of Jesus Christ for the remission of sins; and you shall receive the gift of the Holy Spirit. For the promise is to you and to your children, and to all who are afar off, as many as the Lord our God will call."   Acts 2:38–39

Since not all Christians speak in tongues, where does it leave them in the process of the sanctification of the Holy Spirit? Naturally, it leads them to believe that their sanctification process is second rate, not working in full force. In some church denominations, Christians who don't speak in tongues are encouraged to seek this gift as the evidence of the baptism in the Holy Spirit of promise. What happens when Christians are convinced that they don't have the fullness of God's Spirit working in them because they don't speak in tongues? They go out and seek this additional baptism that is evidenced by speaking in tongues. What happens when Christians seek this additional experience and still don't speak in tongues? Not only do they believe their sanctification process is inferior in comparison to what others have, but now they also feel God has rejected them, since they sought this additional baptism and it was not given.

Why is this such a critical issue in Christian life? If the ministry of the Holy Spirit is the basis for change and growth in the life of the believer, it is imperative for Christians to know that we all share in the same gift. The apostle Paul said that without the Holy Spirit, we are not even one of God's own (Romans 8:9). The Holy Spirit is the common and defining mark that we belong to God.

It is impossible to live the Christian life without the power source of Christianity which is the Holy Spirit. Waiting for something to happen that has already happened causes believers to be indifferent to the reality that is already at work in them. The only thing accomplished by the idea of a two-stage filling of the Holy Spirit is the creation of a divided Christian community. On one hand, you have an inferior brand of Christians, those without the full promise of the Holy Spirit, while on the other hand you have a superior brand of Christians, those who have the complete fullness of the Holy Spirit and are giving evidence of it by the ability to speak in tongues. If it is true that some Christians don't get all of the Holy Spirit's indwelling the first time around, why isn't there any corrective measures given to us in the Scriptures as to why this happens? Additionally, why would God desire half-baptized sons and daughters?

This doesn't mean that the gift of speaking in tongues is not real today. No, it is as real as the other gifts of the Holy Spirit. However, some have this gift and others don't. The issue in regard to speaking in tongues is about differences in gifts, not differences in how the Holy Spirit indwells us. The Christian life by definition is life in the Spirit. Those who don't have the gift of speaking in tongues have other gifts that those who speak in tongues don't have, but we all have the same Holy Spirit who is the source of all the gifts.

It is important to lock down this truth: men are neither the givers of the gift of the Holy Spirit, nor are they the givers of the gifts of the Holy Spirit, nor are they the means for the fruit of the Holy Spirit. The gift, the gifts and fruit of the Holy Spirit are the results of personal faith in Jesus Christ. To make speaking in tongues the determining sign that one has received an additional filling that is not common to all believers is to take the historical miracle at Pentecost out of context. In the initial experience of speaking in tongues, the miracle was not an end in itself, but rather a means to a greater end.

men are neither the givers of the gift of the Holy Spirit, nor are they the givers of the gifts of the Holy Spirit, nor are they the means for the fruit of the Holy Spirit

Without the ability to speak in different languages the world evangelism to which the disciples had been commissioned would have been impossible. In fact, this language miracle was the very thing that was noticed by those who were present on that day in Jerusalem.

> Then they were all amazed and marveled, saying to one another, "Look, are not all these who speak Galileans? And how is it that we hear, each in our own language in which we were born?" Acts 2:7–8

Why is there such confusion with the baptism of the Holy Spirit? I believe the reason for this confusion is that in the initial baptism of the Holy Spirit, the ability to speak in other languages was instantaneous with the receiving of the Holy Spirit of promise (Acts 2:1–4). This occurrence is what makes many believe that this has to be the pattern for all future believers baptized with the Holy Spirit of promise. All must give evidence of this baptism in the same way the disciples experienced it for the first time.

This makes complete sense if you isolate Acts 2:1–4 from the promise of Jesus Christ in Acts 1:8 and the prophecy of Joel referenced in Acts 2:17. In Acts 1:4-8, the Lord Jesus told His disciples to wait for the promise of the Holy Spirit. He told them that when the Holy Spirit came, they would receive power to be His witnesses to the entire world, beginning in Jerusalem, Judea, and Samaria. What would happen? They would *receive power to be His witnesses*.

When Peter explained what they were experiencing, he referred to the prophecy of Joel. In the prophecy of Joel, God would *pour out His Spirit on all flesh, and the sons and daughters would prophesy* (Acts 2:17). What would happen according to the prophecy of Joel? The sons and daughters of God would *prophesy*. Huh . . . this is very interesting. Both the Lord Jesus Christ and the prophet Joel were in agreement that the main characteristic of the Holy Spirit's indwelling would be *prophecy, not speaking in tongues*.

So then, why did they speak in tongues? It should be obvious, but apparently it's not, since great confusion exists concerning this miracle. The miracle was necessitated by the inability of the disciples to speak in other foreign languages. Since they did not have the time to attend the "Jerusalem School of Foreign Languages," the Holy Spirit gave them the ability to speak in different languages not known to them, but known by their audience who needed to hear the good news of the gospel in their own language (Acts 2:7–8). How would the disciples be able to *prophesy* and share the gospel with the world if they only knew one language? The spread of the gospel would have been limited to only those who spoke the language of the disciples. It is clear beyond a shadow of a doubt, that speaking in tongues was a secondary cause in the primary cause of *prophecy*. Both Jesus Christ and the prophet Joel said this would occur with the coming of the Holy Spirit of promise.

When Paul mentions the gifts of the Holy Spirit in 1 Corinthians, he does not single out speaking in tongues from the other gifts as proof that one has received an additional baptism not common to all Christians. What Paul does is to include this gift with all the other gifts of the Holy Spirit. Additionally, not only does he not exclude speaking in tongues from the other gifts of the Holy Spirit, but he identifies it as being one of the lesser gifts.

> Now you are the body of Christ, and members indi-
> vidually. And God has appointed these in the church:
> first apostles, second prophets, third teachers, after that
> miracles, then gifts of healings, helps, administrations,
> varieties of tongues.   1 Corinthians 12:27–28

Telling Christians they don't have the baptism of the Holy Spirit because they don't speak in tongues, does not line up with good biblical interpretation and creates enormous confusion in the body of Christ. We know that God doesn't lead His church in confusion. However, in spiritual warfare confusion is a very potent weapon that always plays well to the schemes of Satan, while competition plays well to the fallen ego of mankind—"my faith is better than your faith". In spiritual warfare, Satan will always strike first at the assurance of our salvation. He wants us to doubt the reality of our relationship with God through Jesus Christ. If he is unable to accomplish this, he will strike at the quality of our salvation, making us think we are inferior in comparison to what other believers have. If Satan is unsuccessful in making us doubt the equality of our son-ship that is lived in the context of diversity, he will target the unity of believers.

This happens when we create our own private interpretations that are for the most part denominational preferences rather than biblical standards. Every Christian has the baptism of the Holy Spirit of promise. The manifestation of that reality differs from one Christian to another for the benefit and edification of the whole body of Christ, a body that functions as a diversity in unity. Paul's purpose in using the analogy of the human body as a picture of the church was to illustrate this point.

> For in fact the body is not one member but many. If the foot should say, "Because I am not a hand, I am not of the body," is it therefore not of the body? And if the ear should say, "Because I am not an eye, I am not of the body," is it therefore not of the body? If the whole body were an eye, where would be the hearing? If the whole were hearing, where would be the smelling? But now God [not men] has set the members, each one of them, in the body just as He pleased [not as it pleased men].
>
> 1 Corinthians 12:14–18, emphasis added

> But the manifestation of the Spirit is given to each one for the profit of all: for to one is given the word of wisdom through the Spirit, to another the word of knowledge through the same Spirit, to another faith by the same Spirit, to another gifts of healings by the same Spirit, to another the working of miracles, to another prophecy, to another discerning of spirits, to another different kinds of tongues, to another the interpretation of tongues. But one and the same Spirit works all these things, distributing to each one

individually as He wills [not as man wills].

1 Corinthians 12:7–11, emphasis added

We don't all have the same gifts, nor does anyone have all the gifts working through them. But we all have the same Holy Spirit who is the source of the gifts being manifested in our lives. What every New Testament born again Christian needs today is to focus on growing in greater intimacy with the Holy Spirit rather than doubting His presence.

Growing Intimacy with the Holy Spirit

Because the Holy Spirit is a person, we can relate to Him in the same way we relate to other individuals we value and desire to get closer to. In fact, the commands given to us in the New Testament regarding the Holy Spirit describe Him as one who can be grieved (Ephesians 4:30), just as we can grieve and sadden the people we love and value most in life. He can be quenched in the same way we can quench the growth in a relationship we value by taking that person for granted (1 Thessalonians 5:19). We can walk with Him in the same way we agree to walk with someone who is going in the same direction we are going (Galatians 5:16). We can be filled with Him in the same way we can give ourselves unconditionally to someone we love (Ephesians 5:18).

These commands regarding the Holy Spirit reveal His personhood, and therefore allow us to embrace Him as we would our best friend. In fact, we should relate to the Holy Spirit in the same way we relate to the people we desire to grow closer to. He is after all the best life companion we can have. Jesus Christ said the Holy Spirit would be the channel by which we would stay spiritually connected and tuned into heaven's resources.

However, when He, the Spirit of truth, has come, *He will guide you into all truth*; for He will not speak on His own authority, but whatever He hears He will speak; and *He will tell you things to come. He will glorify Me,* for *He will take of what is Mine and declare it to you.* All things that the Father has are Mine. Therefore I said that He will take of Mine and declare it to you.   John 16:13–15, emphasis added

According to this passage in John 16, as heaven's ambassador, the Holy Spirit serves four critical functions in the life of the believer in addition to what we have already noted previously.

The Revealer of Truth

First, as heaven's ambassador the Holy Spirit will continue to speak life into us through God's truth: "He will guide you into all truth." What is truth? This question was asked by Pilate over two thousand years ago. From the multibillion-dollar self-help industry, it is evident that mankind is still interested in the question of truth. Some say truth is elusive, until it involves them personally then it's not elusive anymore because everybody wants the truth. You want the truth from your government, you want the truth from the leaders you elect. You want the truth in all your business transactions, whether you are buying a new house or trying out new computer software. You want the truth in your relationships. You want the truth in what defines the good life and the truth about how to pursue it successfully. Everybody needs and wants the truth.

Living in a broken world that doesn't always line up with our wants, it is necessary to hear the truth from God about what really matters most in life. There is a certain agony for all of us who live here on planet earth no one is exempt.

Living in a broken world that doesn't always line up with our wants necessitates hearing the truth from God about what really matters most in life.

Paul called it a "groaning." Creation groans while waiting to be delivered from corruption. God's family groans waiting for the redemption of the body. The Holy Spirit groans as He intercedes for us (Romans 8:19–26). In the midst

of this all-inclusive groaning, it is the truth that comforts us; it is the truth that gives us hope and the truth that keeps us moving forward.

The Revealer of Things to Come

Second, as heaven's ambassador, the Holy Spirit brings us revelation of things to come: "He will tell you things to come." What is the purpose of knowing things to come? There are at least three things to consider; preparedness, protection, and provision. Jesus often spoke to His disciples about the future in order to prepare them and protect them from becoming discouraged through drawing their own conclusions about life. Naturally, when we think about things to come, we have in mind world events leading to the end and the beginning of a new world order (Revelation 21). In this regard, Jesus spoke often of world-changing events that would usher in His return.

However, He did not limit the revelation of "things to come" to only the final end of a new beginning. He also revealed things to come that were closer and more relevant to the disciples' own personal lives. He spoke of the growing opposition of the religious leaders before it happened.

He spoke of His death and resurrection before it happened. He spoke of Judas's betrayal and Peter's denial before it happened. On several occasions He even gave His disciples step-by-step revelation as to what they were to do. When they asked Jesus where He wanted them to prepare the last Passover meal, Jesus gave them a step-by-step prophetic word about going into the city and meeting a man carrying a pitcher of water. They were to follow the man to a house and ask the master of the house where the guest room was. The master of the house would then show them a large room that had been prepared for them (Luke 22:10). Who can deny the advantage of having a life companion who reveals things to come?

The Glorifier of Christ

Third, as heaven's ambassador, the Holy Spirit will never lead us into sinful paths, but only in ways that glorify Christ: "He will glorify Me." It should be noted by all who are concerned that living a life that glorifies Christ is by no means living a pleasure-less ascetic life. This idea that is entertained by many is the exact opposite of what it means to glorify Christ. In glorifying Christ, holiness and pleasure are not two separate issues, in fact, in Christian living they are always together.

You were created in the image of God; therefore, to live in sin is to live in contradiction to your true self. You can, for a short extended time live in contradiction to your true self, but not for the duration of a life time, at least not without severe disappointment. The goal in Christian living is to grow into the fullness of your Christ-identity. This is what will allow you the greatest freedom and self-expression not the restricted life many unfortunately believe. Those who don't live in the fullness of their Christ-identity live in the shadow of the fear and self-doubt that is learned from the experiences of a fallen world. Fear and self-doubt will always cause you to be conquered by life's challenges rather than conquering life's challenges. Conquering life was always God's plan for mankind created in His image.

growing into the fullness of your Christ-identity is what will allow you the greatest freedom and self-expression, not the restricted life many unfortunately believe will happen

Then God blessed them, and God said to them, "Be fruitful and multiply; fill the earth and subdue it; have dominion over the fish of the sea, over the birds of the air, and over every living thing that moves on the earth."   Genesis 1:28

When you live with insecurity, you will always settle for the lesser experience in life. The experiences of the fallen world will always challenge who you are in Christ, your true identity, just like Satan challenged Adam and Eve's true identity in the garden. Life will never be lived better than the vision you have of yourself. When your self-image is distorted, everything else in life will be off center and not work in the way God designed it to work. In biblical terms, when life is lived off center, it is called the "works of the flesh." The works of the flesh can never glorify God because the focus is on living life without acknowledging His goodness and sovereignty.

In Christian life, the goal is to restore life to the authentic true self created in the image of God and for a transparent relationship with God. As such, the process involves a continual realigning of our lives with what is true of us through the redemption that is in Jesus Christ, rather than what is true of us through the experiences of a fallen world.

> I beseech you therefore, brethren, by the mercies of God, that you present your bodies a living sacrifice, holy, acceptable to God, which is your reasonable service. And do not be conformed to this world, but be transformed by the renewing of your mind, that you may prove what is that good and acceptable and perfect will of God. Romans 12:1–2

The process is not as easy as it sounds. In fact, the change in how we perceive ourselves will probably be the deepest level of spiritual warfare we will engage in. Satan does not want us to live out of our true identity. He wants us to live out of the identity that is formed from the experiences of a fallen world. Satan is determined to distort and challenge the truth of our redemption. Nevertheless, it is important not to give into sight, but to have faith in the God who loves us and desires what is the very best for us.

We are adopted sons and daughters through the redemption that is in Jesus Christ. If God is the King of Kings and the Lord of Lords, then as His sons and daughters, we must be princes and princesses living under the authority and character of His name. If such is true, we cannot glorify our Father in heaven by living lives that do not honor His

God the Father wants us to live out our destinies, for through this, we glorify Him by showcasing His love and power to redeem.

authority and character. Believing we are second-class citizens of the world is not living under the adoption of God that comes through Jesus Christ, but rather continuing to live under the curse of the fall. The curse of the fall was removed through the redemption that is in Christ Jesus. God the Father wants us to live out our destinies, for through this we glorify Him by showcasing His love and power to redeem.

> You are the light of the world. A city that is set on a hill cannot be hidden. Nor do they light a lamp and put it under a basket, but ona lampstand, and it gives light to all who are in the house. Let your light so shine before men, that they may see your good works and glorify your Father in heaven. Matthew 5:14–16

The Channel of Blessing

Last, as heaven's ambassador, the Holy Spirit is the one who connects us with all that is God's and communicates it to us: "He will take of what is Mine and declare it to you." In writing to the Christians at Ephesus, Paul described the rich blessings that were theirs through the redemption that is in Jesus Christ. Paul said that they had been blessed with every spiritual blessing in the heavenly places in Christ (Ephesians 1:3). He told them that in past times they were aliens from the commonwealth of God's chosen people, strangers to the covenants of promise, and were without hope and without God, but now through Christ, they were fellow citizens in the household of God (Ephesians 2:1, 12, 19).

God took people who were dead in sin and through Christ made us His very own sons and daughters. Christian life is a calling that connects us to all that is Christ's. For this reason, Peter reminds us that we have been given all things that pertain to life through His power so that we might be partakers of the divine nature (2 Peter 1:3–4). Here is the paradox of Christian living; we are blessed people living in a broken world (Genesis 3). The Christian lives between the fall of Genesis 3 and the complete restoration of Revelation 21. As such, it is impossible to not cross paths with the brokenness of the world, unless we stay home and never come out of our rooms. However, at the same time, it is impossible not to have God's resources to showcase His redemption to a fallen world that needs to see it.

The Holy Spirit will supply heaven's resources so that we can have everything we need to live victoriously as extensions of His kingdom on earth. However, without a growing faith and a growing sensitivity to what is ours through Christ, we can restrict the channel that was designed to communicate God's blessings to us. Don't allow the brokenness of the world to overshadow the truth of God; instead, allow His promises to overshadow the brokenness of the world.

> Never let evil get the best of you; instead, overpower
> evil with the good.   Romans 12:21 VOICE

This was always Paul's main concern as he prayed for his fellow Christians. He obviously felt it was possible for them to overlook the immense riches that were theirs through Christ. In chapter 1 of Ephesians, he prayed that they would grow in wisdom and revelation in the knowledge of God, and that they would know what is the hope of His calling and the riches of the glory of His inheritance in the saints. He prayed that they would embrace the greatness and power that is for all who believe (Ephesians 1:17–19). It is imperative that we always keep this channel of blessing free from the static and interference of the world that keeps us from hearing and receiving from heaven.

The Mandate for all New Testament Believers

In the letter written to the Christians at Ephesus, Paul encouraged his fellow believers to be wise and to make their limited time on earth count for God's purposes. Therefore, he tells them to know what the will of God was for their lives. To avoid needless speculation as to what was the will of God, Paul himself settled the issue for them as well as for us.

> See then that you walk circumspectly, not as fools but as wise, redeeming the time, because the days are evil. Therefore do not be unwise, but understand what the will of the Lord is. And do not be drunk with wine, in which is dissipation; but be filled with the Spirit.
>
> Ephesians 5:15–18

It should not surprise us why Paul encouraged his fellow believers to be filled with the Holy Spirit. In a world in which the choice is between good and evil, our best option is to be influenced and controlled by the Holy Spirit. Why would we consider anything in life of greater value and privilege than to be filled with the Holy Spirit? There is nothing that compares with living the Spirit-filled life. Consider the apostle Peter as an example of the transformation that resulted from a Spirit-filled life. Prior to the Holy Spirit's filling, Peter's life was characterized by highs and lows. He appeared to be the leader among the twelve disciples, and yet, he was the most often rebuked by the Lord Jesus. Peter also appeared to be one who experienced some incredible and unique revelations, and yet on one occasion, the Lord Jesus Himself said to him; "Get behind me, Satan" (Matthew 16:23). Peter at times appeared to be the boldest of the twelve disciples. He was the first to draw his sword at the arrest of Jesus Christ, but then just hours later, denied he even knew Him. Peter's life seemed to be a struggle between what he wished his life would be and the reality that it wasn't. Then there was Pentecost and everything changed in Peter's life.

He was no longer characterized by a life of indecision and cowardice. From that moment he truly became a man of courage and boldness, sure of himself and without wavering. Scripture gives us one simple explanation; Peter and the others were filled with the Holy Spirit (Acts 2:4).

Maintaining the Spirit-Filled Life

The New Testament gives us three commands to maintain Spirit-filled lives. We are not to grieve the Holy Spirit (Ephesians 4:30), we are not to quench the Holy Spirit (1 Thessalonians 5:19), and finally, we are to walk in the Holy Spirit (Galatians 5:17). These three commands reveal that the filling of the

There is a big difference between running after something you don't have and maintaining something you already have.

Holy Spirit is not something elusive to be sought after, but rather something that is to be maintained. There is a big difference between running after something you don't have and maintaining something you already have. The Christian life is lived in the reality of the second option. Maintain what has already been given to you.

Do Not Grieve the Holy Spirit

> And do not grieve the Holy Spirit of God, by whom
> you were sealed for the day of redemption.
>
> Ephesians 4:30

The command not to grieve the Holy Spirit is stated in the negative and implies the positive, by showing us that the Holy Spirit is not someone we have to chase after in order to get filled. He is already a working influence in our lives whom we are commanded not to grieve. We cannot grieve that which we do not have. We can only grieve that which is already a reality in us. *To grieve* is a phrase that communicates intimate closeness and genuine love towards someone. Like a mother, who is deeply saddened by the consequences of poor choices her son or daughter made knowing that better choices were within their reach.

We cannot be grieved by someone we only casually know. The death of someone we casually know may cause us to reflect upon his life, but it will not lead to extended grieving. The only way to be grieved by someone's misfortune is to already be in an intimate relationship with that person.

The Holy Spirit is already in an intimate relationship with all believers and desires to influence our lives in ways that honor God and that lead to consistent blessing; thus the command, "do not grieve the Holy Spirit." Paul's choice of the word *grieve* to describe our relationship with the Holy Spirit is very interesting. Why didn't Paul use a stronger word? For example, why not say, "Don't anger the Holy Spirit," or "Don't you even dare mess with the Holy Spirit if you know what's good for you!" To grieve doesn't communicate the idea that the Holy Spirit is ready to strike us down at the first sign of weakness or disobedience. What it does do, is make Him grieve.

Grieving the Holy Spirit points to whether we will yield to Him in willing surrender. He is not going to force us into submission. He is not a military drill instructor who is going to drive us into submission. He guides and leads us in truth as we follow in willing surrender and submission.

Do Not Quench the Spirit (1 Thessalonians 5:19)

While grieving the Holy Spirit means to sadden Him, quenching the Holy Spirit is willful disobedience. But once again, the fact that it is stated in the negative, "do not quench," implies the positive. You cannot quench what you never had. You must first have it, in order for the possibility to quench it can exist.

While the context in the letter to the Thessalonians was for the most part, a praise offering for the work God was doing in their midst, the latter part of the letter possibly reflects some weariness on the part of some of the members in the congregation. When life is difficult, we all have the tendency to want to take matters into our own hands to end the difficulty as soon as possible. Waiting for things to change for the better is difficult in our microwave culture. In difficult times, it is not uncommon to feel like God has forgotten us, because His answers are slow coming by our timetable.

Perhaps this was Paul's concern for the church at Thessalonica. Paul begins the fifth chapter by making reference to "the day of the Lord" and encouraging them to continue to live as sons of light since they had this great hope. Be watchful and sober, Paul commanded them, do not become slack in the lifestyle that gave testimony of their faith to a watching world. In the verses just before the command not to quench the Spirit, Paul encouraged them to always pursue what was good for them and others (verse 15), to always rejoice (verse 16), to always pray (verse 17), and to always give thanks in everything (verse 18).

Never stop doing these things he said; in other words, "do not quench the Spirit." When trouble comes, it is not the time to quench the one who has been designated to be our comforter and guide in the storms of life. It is the time to be more sensitive in hearing and obeying His voice. Every Christian will face difficult moments; after all, we still live in a fallen world, but the promises we have from God make it worth persevering. In words that Paul would probably say himself, let God *always* have the last word in the outcome of life's challenges.

> And we know that all things work together for good
> to those who love God, to those who are the called
> according to His purpose.   Romans 8:28

Walk in the Holy Spirit

> I say then: Walk in the Spirit, and you shall not fulfill
> the lust of the flesh.   Galatians 5:16

The final command for living a Spirit-filled life is simply to walk in obedience. This command is stated in the positive but implies the negative, as it is possible for a Christian not to walk in obedience. What does it mean to walk in the Spirit? From the physical world, we understand that to walk with someone in a significant and meaningful way, we must first have the desire to go in the same direction the other person is going. Additionally, we must want to arrive at the same destination. If together we are going in the same direction with the desire of arriving at the same destination, the journey will be a pleasant one.

For example, if I ask my younger sister if she would like to go to the mall, her answer will always be yes. She will never resist, in fact, she may even give me directions for the shortest route to the mall. However, if we are forced to walk with someone we don't trust, or if we do not want to go in the same direction the journey will be frustrating to say the least. This leads to a very important question, why does Paul have to command Christians to walk in the Spirit? It almost seems as if Paul is writing to convince Christians who are not sure that the Spirit-filled walk is the best life option. After all, what is the alternative? It's a journey in flesh walking.

> For the flesh lusts against the Spirit, and the Spirit against the flesh; and these are contrary to one another, so that you do not do the things that you wish. But if you are led by the Spirit, you are not under the law. Now the works of the flesh are evident, which are: adultery, fornication, uncleanness, lewdness, idolatry, sorcery, hatred, contentions, jealousies, outbursts of wrath, selfish ambitions, dissensions, heresies, envy, murders, drunkenness, revelries, and the like; of which I tell you beforehand, just as I also told you in time past, that those who practice such things will not inherit the kingdom of God.   Galatians 5:17–21

From verses 17-21, it becomes obvious that every Christian faces the critical decision of being either a Spirit-filled walker or a flesh-filled walker. There is no way to get around it, nor is there any way we can reconcile the two into one life. They are contradictory and incompatible with each other. Why then do Christians struggle back and forth with two choices in life that are so enormously different from each other? It's not as if we are comparing the difference between 999 and 1,000, that's too close to matter and make a difference in how we choose, give me either one.

But the contrast between Holy Spirit living and the works of flesh is so drastically different, it would seem that the choice of walking in the Spirit would be the obvious one. However, such is not the case.

In reality it is here where we struggle the most. The reason being is that the flesh does provide counterfeit ways of meeting legitimate God-given desires that work momentarily, but that in the long run lead to disastrous ends.

> Let no one say when he is tempted, "I am tempted by God"; for God cannot be tempted by evil, nor does He Himself tempt anyone. But each one is tempted when he is drawn away by his own desires and enticed. Then, when desire has conceived, it gives birth to sin; and sin, when it is full-grown, brings forth death.
>
> James 1:13–15

If the desires James says lead to death did not gratify perceived needs, real or unreal (as all behavior is motivated by the gratification of needs), the drive to meeting these needs would lessen. Let's be realistic. The strength of temptation over us lies in our believing that if we don't do what the impulses of the flesh

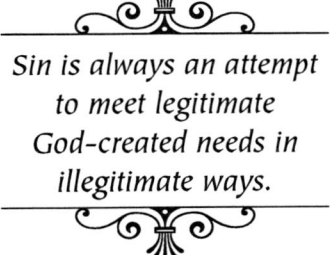

Sin is always an attempt to meet legitimate God-created needs in illegitimate ways.

are urging us to do, our basic needs in life will go unmet. Sin is always an attempt to meet legitimate God-created desires in illegitimate ways. No Christian wakes up in the morning and says; "This is a great day to sin." No one ever thinks it's a perfect day for committing adultery and shaming and ruining their marriage and possibly their family. No one ever wakes up in the morning thinking it's a perfect day to practice immorality. No one is that dull of mind to do things like this, yet it happens all the time.

Why do we allow this to happen? When we don't trust God to meet our needs, we turn to the counterfeit methods found in the flesh.

That is what the flesh is; a reliance on self as opposed to a reliance on God, who James says is the giver of good and perfect gifts (James 1:17). If Abraham Maslow, American psychologist best known for creating the "hierarchy of human needs" would have lived in the Garden of Eden, he would have noted that all of Adam and Eve's hierarchal needs where adequately met. However, when there is no faith or reliance in the goodness of God, the reliance to meet needs in a fallen world turns self-ward, to the flesh.

Life's Fantastic Four

Sexuality, Worship, Identity, and Empowerment

> Now the works of the flesh are evident, which are: adultery, fornication, uncleanness, lewdness, idolatry, sorcery, hatred, contentions, jealousies, outbursts of wrath, selfish ambitions, dissensions, heresies, envy, murders, drunkenness, revelries, and the like; of which I tell you beforehand, just as I also told you in time past, that those who practice such things will not inherit the kingdom of God.   Galatians 5:19–21

Counterfeit Sexuality

Adultery

Fornication

Uncleanness

Lewdness

The sexual behaviors Paul notes in Galatians chapter 5 was not to show us God is anti-sex, but rather to contrast false sexuality with true sexuality. God is not anti-sex, you will not go to hell or anger God for having sexual desires. In fact, God was the creator of your sexual desires through the creation of male and female.

However, as the designer of our sexuality Father knows best. For the sexual experience to be a blessing in the life of a man and a woman, it must follow the instruction manual of the One who created it. If it doesn't, the pleasure of a sexual experience can become an experience of regret and shame that will most certainly outlast a physical orgasm. God never intended sex to end in a hex. He intended it to be pleasurable while at the same time being purposeful. The power of our sexuality can either build up a strong healthy society or destroy it—that's how powerful it is. As such, God's will for our sexuality is that it be expressed inside a marriage covenant where there is a lifetime commitment between male and female.

God's plan for marriage was to create a oneness between a man and woman that is reflected spiritually, intellectually, emotionally, materially, and physically. In human relationships there is no greater relationship than marriage. When the marriage succeeds, all ramifications of societal order succeed. Paul commanded husbands to love their wives as Christ loved the church and gave Himself for it. Wives are commanded to submit to their husbands as unto the Lord (Ephesians 5:22–25). No other relationships in life are given these commands as the basis for relating. For this reason it is easy to conclude that adultery, fornication, uncleanness, and lewdness are nothing more than methods of reducing people to mere objects of consumption, rather than viewing them as being created in the image of God with great eternal value and purpose.

When sex is viewed only as a product of consumption, it results in all kinds of abuses against human beings created in the image of God. Usually with women absorbing the greatest disadvantage. Contrary to popular opinion; pregnancy is never an accident, it is by divine design. What happens when human beings are created in the act of sex but then abandoned when they come into this world? They have to somehow learn to survive on their own. Those who do survive abandonment learn how to survive it in the streets. Street survival usually means a survival of the fittest. Children raised in the streets usually grow up with no love or respect for self, others, or for authority. It's not because they were born this way, but because unprotected children are most vulnerable and become prey to the exploitation of a fallen world. Life in the streets is cheap, and those who grow up in the streets usually think of themselves as cheap too.

Counterfeit Worship (worth-ship)

Idolatry
Sorcery

The idolatry and sorcery Paul mentions are sins against true worship. Human beings, by their finiteness and by their great complexity are a reflection of something greater than themselves, and subsequently worshipers by nature. Our worship defines that which is greater than ourselves and at the same time, defines what is worth pursuing with all our might. The most common form of worship today is self-worship, meaning that we don't adhere to a belief in a higher power. We are gods ourselves and create our own destinies through our own strength and intellect. Others who acknowledge the absurdity of this kind of thinking seek meaning and purpose beyond themselves.

Life, as we experience it necessitates a Creator. When we look into the firmament, it points to a reality beyond ourselves. For this reason, the most intelligent scientist in the world today cannot answer the most innocent intellectual curiosity of a first-grader who asks, "Why do I exist?" Answering the question of what happens scientifically, doesn't answer the question of why it happened when it need not to have happened in the first place. Answering both questions is necessary for any claim towards intelligent humanity.

This provides us with some clarity when it comes to the issue of true worship. Obviously we cannot worship ourselves since we are finite, mortal, and diminishing. What great benefit is there in worshiping ourselves? We also cannot worship other humans since they are flawed with the same propensities we all have. We cannot worship inanimate objects such as mountains, rocks, or sticks, nor can we worship animals or insects since we are the highest form of intelligent life on planet earth. We also cannot worship fallen spiritual creatures, in spite of the fact that they may be superior to humans, they do not reflect the goodwill God has towards beings created in His image. In life, everyone looks for something on which to anchor life. Meaning and purpose in life require something or someone bigger than ourselves to which we look for the explanation of our own existence. God is both the "what" and the "why" of life and the only one who deserves our true worship.

> For in Him we live and move and have our being, as also some of your own poets have said, "For we are also His offspring." Acts 17:28

Counterfeit Identity

Hatred

Contentions

Jealousies

Wrath

Selfish Ambitions

Dissension

Heresies

Envy

Murders

The emotions and behaviors described by Paul are sins against our true personhood. Without truth in this very critical part of life that defines who we are, we will begin to live out of a counterfeit self that manifests itself in false thoughts. False thinking always leads to false feelings; and false feelings always lead to false behavior. Let me take some liberty in categorizing these behaviors of the flesh. Hatred, contentions, jealousies, outbursts of anger, and envy all come from a sense of insecurity that is based on a false identity.

In reality, no one is really inferior in comparison to anyone else. We are all just tailor-made different for the purpose of fulfilling God's purpose in our lives. Our true identity and true worth in life come from God Himself and from fulfilling His calling on our lives, not from how well we fare in comparison to others. When we feel insecure through comparing ourselves with others, we usually respond with competitiveness in order to prove our significance to people who have nothing to do with how our lives turn out. Many times what happens is that we get so busy in trying to be like others or trying to prove our worth, we miss out on our own special calling in life. The only thing that is accomplished by comparing and competing with others is that we usually end up hating ourselves as well as others. Self-worth that is based upon how well we compare with others just leads to more insecurity and the behavior Paul listed as works of the flesh.

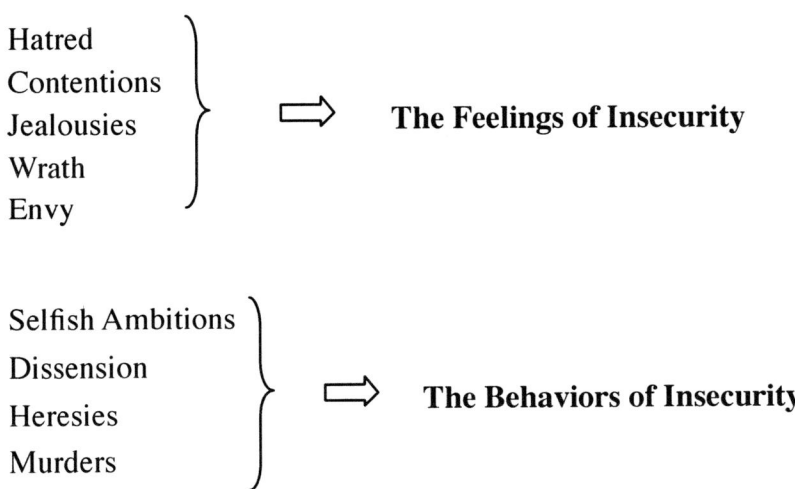

Hatred
Contentions
Jealousies
Wrath
Envy
⇨ **The Feelings of Insecurity**

Selfish Ambitions
Dissension
Heresies
Murders
⇨ **The Behaviors of Insecurity**

Counterfeit Empowerment

Drunkenness
Revelries

Drunkenness and revelries are sins against true empowerment. Living life where there is no faith in the providence and goodness of God, and where every man and woman is competing in a survival of the fittest will most certainly produce more losers than winners. This will require coping and empowerment mechanisms to deal with life's losses and to give oneself a better opportunity to win and stay on top. This is what the alcoholic and drug cultures have become. No child would ever say: "When I grow up, I would like to be a drug addict or an alcoholic." No one lives a substance-abuse lifestyle simply for the purpose of creating a chemically induced experience that contradicts healthy life practices. Most often these activities are sought in the absence of the empowerment that comes from living out of one's true identity.

In the absence of real and authentic empowerment, people often use counterfeits to create a sense of wellness or empowerment that is missing in life. Life-altering substances are usually used for the following reasons:

1. They can be used as an empowerment mechanism for people who lack proper and healthy self-esteem.

2. They can also be used as a coping-mechanism or for self-medicating purposes when people don't know how to move beyond the hurt and disappointments of life's setbacks.

3. They can be used as a social lubricant for life situations that make us feel uncomfortable. Being under the influence of mood-altering substances can relieve the stress of being in social situations that make us feel uncomfortable.

4. They are often used as a sign of coming of age. Young people drink socially because there is in it a false symbolism that means they have passed from adolescence into adulthood. Social drinking is a sort of unwritten cultural badge indicating a person is all grown up. It's a freedom statement. Obviously young people don't get caught up in this cultural phenomenon because they have given it extreme contemplation, weighing in all the pros and cons and coming to the conclusion that yes indeed, their lives will be much more meaningful by their

choosing to be a social or recreational drinker. Young people drink because they get caught up in this unwritten cultural rule of life and don't even realize they are being hijacked by it until it's too late. That's what you are supposed to do when you're all grown up, they think.

Truth be known, you don't have to cave into this delusion. Contrary to popular opinion, your life will not fall into an abyss of meaninglessness as a result of choosing to live sober. Your liver will also love you for it. For those who struggle with defining maturity, perhaps you need to be reminded that the greater maturity in life is when you don't need to rely in these life-altering substances to create or enhance what's really missing. For many, what's really missing in life is the empowerment that comes from knowing that the God of the universe is also our heavenly Father through the redemption that is in Jesus Christ. That is all the empowerment you will ever need in life.

5. Finally, sometimes people use drugs and alcohol to counter the boredom in life that usually comes from a lack of real purpose. The greatest high in life comes from purpose as we shall see in the next chapter.

Alcohol, Wine, and the Christian

Is it evil to celebrate life's successes, life's meaningful events with a little wine or some other alcoholic beverage? I don't think there is anything in the Bible that would prohibit such usage. What I think is clearly prohibited in Scripture is using alcohol as an empowerment or coping device in an attempt to substitute the life empowerment that comes from a growing relationship with God. God is our true source of life empowerment, our true source of coping, and our true source of victory in all of life's challenges.

The Counterfeit Always Implies the Real

The false always implies the real and authentic. Our sexuality, worship, identity, and life-empowerment are extremely important aspects of human life. They are the parts and pieces of life that make up the totality of what it means to be a human being and therefore cannot be left to chance. God is the one who defines what healthy sexuality is for our highest good and pleasure. God is the source of our true identity. He is the object of our worship and the means of our true life-empowerment.

We all live abundantly well or progressively miserable in proportion to what we believe is true about God and ourselves. For this reason Paul says that those who practice the works of the flesh cannot inherit the kingdom of heaven (Galatians 5:21). Their behavior reflects a complete denial of trust in the goodness and providence of God. They live entirely from a self-centered approach to life rather than from a God-centered approach to life. That is what it means to live in the flesh.

To walk in the Holy Spirit means to trust that where He is leading is the very best for us. When we believe this is true, we don't resist walking step by step with the Holy Spirit as our guide. We cooperate to the fullest extent, nothing in our walk is done grudgingly or with second-guessing in our hearts. When we don't trust the Holy Spirit we cannot walk in willing obedience, but rather, we live in the anxiety that our needs will not be met. In that instance we settle for the flesh alternative. We take matters into our own hands. We give in to the voice that whispers in our ear, "God is taking too long", and your needs are not being met. You deserve to have your needs met right now. This is what Satan whispered into the ear of Eve: "You can have it all right now, the moment you act outside of God's declared will."

There are two basic reasons why we get caught up in walking in the flesh instead of walking in the Spirit. The first reason is that we really don't trust God to meet our needs; the second reason is that the flesh does provide an alternative that seems to work momentarily. In the beginning the works of the flesh do produce a sense of wellness in which we feel physically and emotionally alive and satisfied, but then all hell breaks loose in our lives. It should be noted that God did not create us with all of our God-given instincts in order to frustrate us. However, He does want us to trust Him to meet the deepest desires of our hearts better than we can meet them ourselves.

> The eyes of all look expectantly to You, and You give them their food in due season. You open Your hand and satisfy the desire of every living thing.
>
> Psalm 145:15–16

What Sanctification Means in Everyday Life

The Holy Spirit who is present in the life of all believers means that there are certain internal promptings we all share in common, even though our spiritual gifts and ministries may differ from one another. It is through the Holy Spirit that we receive a new nature, one that is continually growing into the image of Jesus Christ.

New Sensitivity Towards Sin

The born again experience explains why we no longer feel comfortable living in the sins of the past. When we sin, we feel a deep inner discomfort that we didn't feel before. It is like going without bathing after a busy, sweaty day of working in the yard. When my eighteen-year-old son came home from his summer job, it was the same routine every day; he greeted his grandparents, greeted his dog, said "Hi, Dada," and headed straight for the shower. No one would ever think of putting on clean clothes before bathing. In the same way we don't feel okay in a dirty, smelly body, it is the same in the spiritual realm. When the Holy Spirit invades our lives, we are no longer okay with sin. It doesn't mean we will never sin again, but no one can be a real born again Christian and be okay with sin.

This is not to imply that people who are not born again are not moral or that they don't feel any guilt after committing acts that are morally wrong. All people feel a sense of obligation to a moral code. It is the evidence that we were all created in the image of a holy, moral God. The difference however, I believe is twofold: First, the Christian is going to experience greater sorrow for anything that contradicts the nature of God that is now in him through the presence of the Holy Spirit. People who are not born again will experience guilt, but the guilt will most likely be a passing guilt and not endure to the point of confession and repentance towards God. This is because life without the Holy Spirit is self-centered rather than God-centered.

Second, I believe the motivation of a person filled with the Holy Spirit differs from a person living without the born again experience. In Christian life, the inward bent is never to fall or give into temptation, whereas the goal in a person who does not have the Holy Spirit may simply be not to get caught and thus avoid consequences. It's okay to err occasionally from the higher standard, as long as you don't get caught and there is mutual agreement. The idea that it's okay to do something that is morally wrong as long as no one gets hurt is part of the fallen nature that is driven by self-gratification, rather than living with faith in the goodness of God who meets our needs better than we can meet them ourselves.

Through the Holy Spirit we become attracted to the light of Christ and loathe the darkness that is in the world and in us. Our thoughts, feelings, and behavior begin to change. Our speech and habits begin to change. The way we think about life in general begins to change. We no longer live in the flow and current of the world where the goal in life is to make it to the top at any cost. We now live with a real sense of destiny that involves being an extension of God's kingdom purpose. Our worldview begins to line up with the life reflected in Jesus Christ. He becomes the pattern in all we do in life. We become born again through the Holy Spirit (John 3).

God's Word Becomes an Open Book

Through the Holy Spirit, the Bible which is our main source of spiritual nourishment becomes an open book. It no longer remains closed to our understanding, nor is it thought of as a boring outdated book. No one can be born again and remain indifferent towards the Word of God. On the contrary, it becomes the primary channel we tune in to, in order to hear the voice of God. It becomes the source of our joy, full of meaning, purpose, and the standard by which we interpret life. As one of my colleagues would say; it becomes the meat and potatoes of those who are spiritually hungry for something more out of life. God's Word becomes our compass through life's journey, our "how to" instruction book for all of life's concerns. The apostle Peter said, "As newborn babes, desire the pure milk of the word, that you may grow thereby, if indeed you have tasted that the Lord is gracious" (1 Peter 2:2–3).

Character Growth and Development

It is through the sanctification in the Holy Spirit that the character of Christ begins to form in us. Paul lists nine characteristics of the fruit of the Spirit in Galatians 5. The fact that Paul mentions nine qualities is by no means conveying the idea that a Christian may have more growth in one area over another. For example, would it be possible for a Christian to have love, but then fall short in the other areas of the Spirit's qualities? Obviously, this would present multiple options and in the end produce ineffective Christians in the relational domain of life. A Christian who loves but has no patience would be contradictory to say the least. For this reason, it is important to notice that these qualities of the Holy Spirit Paul mentions are called the *fruit* of the Spirit, not the *fruits* (plural) of the Spirit. The fruit of the Holy Spirit manifests itself in nine qualities that make us inwardly beautiful and powerful over comers in life. All are being produced in us simultaneously as we walk in obedience.

> But the fruit of the Spirit is love, joy, peace, longsuf-
> fering, kindness, goodness, faithfulness, gentleness,
> self-control. Against such there is no law.
> Galatians 5:22–23

While the fruit of the Spirit is for the purpose of empowering us internally, specifically with regards to how well we live with self and others, the gifts of the Spirit are for the purpose of empowering us for service — first, in the context of the church, and then in the wider context of a world that needs to see the love and power of God.

> There are diversities of gifts, but the same Spirit.
> There are differences of ministries, but the same
> Lord. And there are diversities of activities, but it is

the same God who works all in all. But the manifestation of the Spirit is given to each one for the profit of all: for to one is given the word of wisdom through the Spirit, to another the word of knowledge through the same Spirit, to another faith by the same Spirit, to another gifts of healings by the same Spirit, to another the working of miracles, to another prophecy, to another discerning of spirits, to another different kinds of tongues, to another the interpretation of tongues. But one and the same Spirit works all these things, distributing to each one individually as He wills [not as man wills, because it is not his to give].   1 Corinthians 12:4–11

Paul commands Christians to be filled with the Holy Spirit. Do not grieve or quench the Holy Spirit. Walk in obedience to the Holy Spirit knowing that He is not indifferent toward your deepest desires. He created them with the intention of fulfilling them in His perfect timing. Walking in the Spirit is trusting God knows you better than you know yourself and that He is leading you to a greater end than you could never accomplish by yourself.

Chapter 6

Life's Greatest Purpose
(Why God Calls Everyone)

C oming into the family of God is more than just punching your one-way ticket to heaven. Redemption also includes a kingdom assignment that becomes your personal life journey. In the family of God, everyone gets involved and becomes an extension of God's work on planet earth. Your life becomes a living testimony to others of God's unconditional love and power to redeem. For this reason, it is important to know that living in your calling is just as important as what God is doing in your life through the other parts of redemption. It cannot be something you overlook or something that is looked upon with lesser value. In fact, your kingdom purpose is the key to your life fulfillment.

It is very unfortunate that many of God's children miss out on life's true fulfillment because they ignore this very important part of redemption. Perhaps the reason we miss out is that calling has been limited to the traditional roles we see inside a church building. Without calling, God's people have nowhere to land except to default to pursuing the same things non-Christians seek for life fulfillment.

Erik Rees says: "People tend to define their purpose in life by one of three things; trends, what others tell them, or by truth. When we let trends guide our life, we simply are living to fit into the current styles of the world. When we let others tell us what we should be doing, we are living to please them and win their approval. However, when we let God's truth define our Kingdom Purpose, submitting to His authority and desiring to please only Him, we are able to lead a life of lasting significance, fulfillment, and Kingdom impact."[7]

Contrary to popular opinion, we were not created for stuff, but for eternal purpose. Think about it, if you always need the new or advanced version of the same things you already have, then obviously those things did not lead to the fulfillment you thought they would bring. And neither will the new things you have now for they too will be replaced by next year's new advanced version. John Ortberg, in his book, *You Can't Take It with You,* says: "We all have stuff. We see it, want it, buy it, display it, insure it, and compare it with other people's stuff. We talk about whether or not they have too much stuff; we envy or pass judgment on other people's collections of stuff. We collect our own little pile. We imagine that if that pile got big enough, we would feel successful or secure. That's how you keep score in Monopoly, and that's how our culture generally keeps score as well."[8]

Without kingdom purpose, life eventually becomes a routine of accumulating things that ultimately end up in the garage collecting dust or in a self-storage building. John Ortberg says: "We now spend $12 billion a year just to pay someone to store our extra stuff. It's larger than the music industry."[9] Jesus said, "Do not lay up for yourselves treasures on earth, where moth and rust destroy and where thieves break in and steal; but lay up for yourselves treasures in heaven, where neither moth nor rust destroys and where thieves do not break in and steal" (Matthew 6:19–20). To people whose passion in life was riches, the Lord Jesus pointed them to the riches that were eternal not temporal.

Living life with purpose is a big part of God's redemption. Louie Giglio says in *I Am Not But I Know I AM:* "Life is a tale of two stories, one finite and frail, the other eternal and enduring. The tiny one, the story of us, is as brief as the blink of an eye. Yet somehow our infatuation with our own little story and our determination to make it as big as we possibly can, blinds us to the massive God story that surrounds us on every side."[10] Fulfillment that is based on purpose will always be greater than fulfillment that is based on the accumulation of things. Everything that is under the control of God grows and becomes a life-giving source.

Myles Munroe says in *Releasing Your Potential*: "Each of us comes into this world with an assignment to fulfill. God commissions us to leave for the following generations something from which they can learn and be inspired."[11] Deep down in the heart of every man and woman, it's not enough to just be physically alive. Deep down, everyone wants to make a contribution. The truth is, the greatest inspiration in our lives does not come from stuff, but from other human beings like us. We too have been redeemed to show His great love and power to restore and create great purpose out of broken lives.

The world is waiting to hear your redemption story and waiting for your special purpose to inspire and motivate others to go forward and trust God just as you did. When you live out your calling, you will be fulfilled, your calling will bless others, and God will be glorified.

Calling an Integral Part of Our Redemption

Every human who has been redeemed comes into redemption with a past he or she is not specifically proud of; a past where we have not only been on the receiving side of the world's brokenness, but also on the giving side of it. This is the way life operates in a fallen world. Sooner or later we all end up on both sides. This is what often creates an unending cycle of continued brokenness in the lives of those who refuse Christ's invitation of redemption.

For those who have accepted God's redemption through Christ, the calling of their redemption serves as the means to heal the past. In justification God redeems our past, in calling God redeems our future. To highlight this aspect of God's incredible redemption consider the parable of the prodigal son in Luke 15.

In the parable, the younger son left his father in order to live a more self-directed approach to life. His assumption was that far from home he would experience greater life fulfillment. However, the glamorous life he thought would result from breaking free from home life soon turned chaotic, as this young man runs out of money and real friends. In this diminished and depleted state of life, he was forced into two choices: die in bitter shame, or humbly return home and admit he had been wrong. With deep guilt and shame, he starts homeward hoping that his father would find it in his heart to forgive him and perhaps allow him to live as one of the hired servants.

As he returns, his father sees him from a distance. The father felt compassion towards his erring son and begins to run toward him. When the father reached him, he fell all over his erring son and begins to kiss him. The father instructs his servants to immediately begin the process of re-dressing his son. He commanded them to bring a robe for his covering, a ring, and sandals. Additionally, he commanded the servants to bring the fatted calf and prepare for a great celebration. What was the celebration about? The father himself declared it: "My son was dead and is alive again, he was lost but now is found" (Luke 15:24).

What would have happened if the son's expectation of his father's actions would have been accurate upon his return? What if upon his son's return, the father had said, "I forgive you, but because of your deliberate disrespect you will not return as my son, but only as one of my hired servants," as the son had anticipated? What if the father had said, "Your dwelling place will be among the servants. You will eat when they eat, and live where they live."

If this scenario had taken place, the prodigal son would have avoided sudden death for sure, but what about his dignity? He would have lived the rest of his life with regret and shame, perhaps even later entertaining suicidal thoughts. Every day he would have woken up only to remember what used to be his and how foolish he had been with his choices. Every day he would have woken up and perhaps heard whispers behind him: "He used to be the master's son, our future master, but now he works side by side with the very servants he was destined to rule over." What a tremendous burden to his spiritual and psychological makeup if he had been made to live the rest of his life with only regret and shame. However, this is not the way the parable ends.

The story progresses through great forgiveness, great restoration, great celebration, and great destiny as the younger son is received back and restored into full sonship. That is the significance of the robe, ring, sandals, and the celebration. They are symbolic of the total redemption, the extreme makeover and the son's reinstatement into his father's business. What is the application of the prodigal son's reinstatement to our own redemption story? It is the same; God has received us into full sonship through Jesus Christ regardless of our past and because of this, we have been called into the Father's kingdom business.

God never redeems without calling. Your calling is what creates new experiences that become your new reference point to the past. Without redemption's calling, you would only have the memories of the past and the regret and shame connected to it. God, however, is not only concerned with your forgiveness, but also with restoring your dignity and purpose in life. It becomes clear that living in your calling is God's way of healing your past, so that your past life is not some kind of evil ghost in your closet reminding you of what you used to be.

But what if you consider yourself someone who hasn't had a prodigal son experience? In that case, it is a wonderful thing that you have been able to escape the pollution of the world. But have you been able to escape the pollution of self-righteousness? In my experience in ministry, when someone doesn't necessarily fit the description of the younger son, there is the example of the older brother who stayed home as a silent prodigal. Both sons were prodigals in different ways; the younger through living in a distant land was far from his father's will. The older, although never leaving home, was distant from the father's true heart. This was immediately revealed when the younger brother returned home. The older brother wanted justice and condemnation for his little brother. Religious people are often the quickest to judge sinners and demand immediate justice and punishment before they seek to understand the brokenness that led them toward their reckless behavior. Religious people are often in greater darkness because their darkness is masked in religious activities. In this sense, the older prodigal who stayed home was at greater risk.

Maybe, like the older son, you have a need to know your heavenly Father better and to know that He never desires the punishment of sinners, but grants mercy, grace, and empowerment to all. He calls us to Himself to work in His kingdom business, and in doing so, He not only redeems us from the past, but redeems us for a future. To live unengaged in your calling is to miss out on the fulfillment part of your redemption and puts you at risk to return to your past way of life. Many individuals who don't continue to progress in sanctification do so because they fail to embrace God's calling in their lives. Real change requires not only embracing the truth that sets us free, but a new life mission that supports new life behaviors.

1. God's calling is the key to your fulfillment.
2. God's calling is the key to healing your past.
3. God's calling is the key to avoiding entanglement with unfruitful works.
4. God's calling is the key to blessing others.
5. God's calling is the key for glorifying God and moving others towards redemption.

Misconceptions About Calling—Only Clergy Need Apply

It is not uncommon in the church today to have the idea that calling is limited to the ministry of a pastor, evangelist, missionary, or perhaps to the leadership roles that are necessary in the organization of the church. If this is true, at least it explains why so many of the few called ones are overworked, frustrated, and completely exhausted. This is the outcome when only a few are doing all the work and the rest are just watching. It also explains why so many Christians live unfulfilled lives.

Christianity was never intended to be lived out as a spectator, it is not one of the gifts or fruit of the Spirit. All the gifts of the Holy Spirit are for the purpose of getting involved in the local church. Paul reminded the church at Ephesus in chapter 4 that God called some to be apostles, prophets, evangelists, pastors, and teachers for equipping the saints for the work of ministry (Ephesians 4:11–12). This verse clearly shows that the ministry of church leaders is to train the body of Christ for the work of the ministry. It may be in the expansion of the kingdom of God, the edification of the kingdom of God, or the organization of the kingdom of God. Everyone is called of God to be involved in some capacity.

I'm Not Worthy to Be Called

Some individuals have the false idea that they are not worthy of any calling from God. To believe God cannot use your life for His glory is to devalue what happened at the cross and to reduce God to the image of man. God is much bigger than your past. His love and forgiveness are also much bigger than yours. If God has forgiven you, you should forgive yourself too and move into your kingdom assignment. To live with un-forgiveness toward yourself is to fail to acknowledge that Christ's sacrifice on the cross was greater than your sin. Isn't that the main point in the parable of the prodigal son? The younger son, the father forgave and restored into full sonship; the older son, he invited to know him better by reminding him that all that was the father's was also his; "All that I have is yours" (Luke 15:31).

How necessary it is to be reminded that all that belongs to God the Father is ours too through the adoption we have through Jesus

Christ? We need to be reminded of this very truth every day of our lives until we start believing it and reflecting it in the way we live our lives. Feeling unworthy to be used for God's purposes is not something that comes from the Holy Spirit, but from the enemy who seeks to steal, kill, and destroy (John 10:10).

Calling and Fulfillment—Separate Issues

Perhaps some individuals shy away from their calling because they have been falsely convinced that calling and personal life fulfillment are separate issues. In this particular way of understanding God's will for your life, you must choose between one or the other. You must choose to pursue God's calling and sacrifice your personal life fulfillment, or you must choose your personal life fulfillment at the cost of ignoring God's calling. Nothing could be further from the truth. In fact, your calling is the key to both glorifying God and finding personal life fulfillment. Contrary to popular opinion, the two are not separate issues. In the will of God, calling and fulfillment are always together.

> You will show me the path of life; in Your presence is fullness of joy; at Your right hand are pleasures for-evermore.   Psalm 16:11

Calling Is Being Busy

On the opposite extreme of being a Christian spectator is the idea of doing as much as you can, as often as you can, for as long as you can. Being involved in every ministry and activity in the church may impress the people around you, but it is not the way God calls you to serve Him. I remember many years ago attending a pastors' conference in which one of the training sessions was titled "How to Avoid Burnout." I thought this was an odd way of listing the training session in light of the fact that Jesus said He had come to lift our burdens, not weigh us down in them. If you are tired and close to reaching burnout, you're probably doing more than what you were called to do. Perhaps you are living with a false sense of guilt that is driving you to go nonstop; "I love Jesus, so please get out of my way," Jesus said:

> Come to Me, all you who labor and are heavy laden, and I will give you rest. Take My yoke upon you and learn from Me, for I am gentle and lowly in heart, and you will find rest for your souls. For My yoke is easy and My burden is light.   Matthew 11:28–30

Being in God's perfect will leads to rest and peace while you are in the work. It will never lead to a weight heavier than you can carry. God will never call you to do something He doesn't equip you for. This doesn't mean there will never be difficult days. Our common enemy opposes us every step of the way. However, Jesus said all authority was given to Him in heaven and earth. This truth and promise is sufficient for us to continue in His work, knowing that our work in the Lord is not in vain.

The Prosperity Gospel

The phrase *"Thy will be done"* was spoken in response to the disciples' request to have Jesus teach them how to pray. It would be difficult, perhaps even impossible, for this kind of praying to have any appeal in the hearts of our narcissistic society. Perhaps the greater surprise is that this kind of praying doesn't have much appeal either to the new brand of Christian, who has been convinced that the focus in Christian living is all about them rather than about a kingdom, God's kingdom. Let's be realistic—if there's money in the bank and everyone is healthy, many times church attendance is just another activity demonstrating social status. Very few people attend church with the expectation that God will interfere in the fulfilling of their own desires and dreams. On the contrary, we often hold Him accountable in playing a significant role in the realization of our own personal goals.

The critical question in the issue of personal life fulfillment, as noted earlier, is not one about personal preference—*How much of the world's treasure can I accumulate before I die?*— but one of essence—*Who am I at the core of my being?* The answer to this question is by far the one with the greater value because we cannot live in contradiction to what we were created to be and still live a fulfilling life with any consistency. If you desire to be fulfilled in your life, as one of my colleagues would say, "you have to stay in your lane." In traffic, not only is staying in your lane the law, but crossing over at the wrong time can definitely result in the wrong choice.

Overlooking your calling in life will cause you to miss out on the fulfillment God created you to experience. Perhaps someone may challenge and oppose this way of thinking by reminding us that the disciples were beaten, thrown in prison, and all but one died a martyr's death in pursuing the will of God. How can that be fulfilling? Here's how: purpose that exceeds the span of our lives will always prove to be the greater fulfillment in life. We know nothing of the men who martyred the disciples, we don't even know their names. Their lives have passed into obscurity lost in history. The death they brought upon the disciples was insignificant compared with the power of influence they still have today in the lives of believers.

On the other side, the life absorbed in self is what often creates the greatest emptiness and regret. Consider Solomon as a case study. He always had more than what he needed, but never enough of what he really needed. The Solomon syndrome continues today in the lives of many who have an abundance of things but fail to have an abundance of life.

> So I became great and excelled more than all who were before me in Jerusalem. Also my wisdom remained with me. Whatever my eyes desired I did not keep from them. I did not withhold my heart from any pleasure, for my heart rejoiced in all my labor; and this was my reward from all my labor. Then I looked on all the works that my hands had done; and on the labor in which I had toiled; and indeed all was vanity and grasping for the wind. There was no profit under the sun.   Ecclesiastes 2:9–11

How true it is that nothing in this world after experiencing it for the first time, can keep on fascinating us like it did the first time. And the quality of things fade into nothing in the routine of daily life. For this reason Solomon said:

> Therefore I hated life because the work that was done under the sun was distressing to me, for all is vanity and grasping for the wind.   Ecclesiastes 2:17

A Biblical Definition of Prosperity

Perhaps in our search and desire for a fulfilling life, we need a new definition of prosperity, one that is actually according to the Holy Scriptures.

> Now godliness with contentment is great gain. For we
> brought nothing into this world, and it is certain we
> can carry nothing out. And having food and clothing,
> with these we shall be content. But those who desire
> to be rich fall into temptation and a snare, and into
> many foolish and harmful lusts which drown men in
> destruction and perdition. For the love of money is a
> root of all kinds of evil, for which some have strayed
> from the faith in their greediness, and pierced them-
> selves through with many sorrows. 1 Timothy 6:6–10

Contrary to what you may have heard, the pursuit of things will not automatically result in a fulfilling life. Often what does result is an enslavement to a materialistic way of life in which we live only for the temporal and forget about what lasts forever. Buying into the ideology that quantity makes quality often leads us to being trapped in jobs we hate in order to keep up with what the world defines as success. To pursue wealth as the primary objective in Christian living, is not in line with the heart and mind of Jesus who had His own definition of success.

> Do not lay up for yourselves treasures on earth, where
> moth and rust destroy and where thieves break in and
> steal; but lay up for yourselves treasures in heaven,
> where neither moth nor rust destroys and where
> thieves do not break in and steal. Matthew 6:19–20

Paul told the Christians in Rome that they were not to be conformed to this world, but rather, they were to be transformed by the renewing of their minds to the end of knowing what was the good and perfect will of God (Romans 12:2). The goal of Christian living is not to become rich, but to know the perfect will of God. We are to be transformed in our thinking to the point of embracing His desires and dreams as our own. This transformation of the mind is not simply for the purpose of acknowledging God's rule over us, but for acknowledging that His will for our lives is the best of all possible worlds.

You do not have a better plan for life than what God has planned for you. Embracing His desires and dreams is the key to your fulfillment in life. That is what it means to be a disciple of Christ. Paul said he no longer lived, but Christ lived through him (Galatians 2:20). There is no better meditation in the heart and mind of man than to dwell on "Thy will be done." There is no better activity for man than to be active in expanding his purpose, "Thy kingdom come," unless, of course, he is smarter than God. Don't waste your life trying to be smarter than God, no one really is. Instead, live your life in the way God designed it.

Does this mean that we are not to have any wealth at all? Of course not. God created human life with both spiritual and physical dimensions. Being a Christian doesn't mean you don't need a place to live or a car to take you from point A to point B. In the prayer Jesus gave to His disciples, He did not separate the spiritual from the material. He connected them, acknowledging what it means to be a total human being. In doing so, He made it clear that He cares about meeting our daily needs.

Nevertheless, it is extremely clear from the Lord's Prayer that there is a spiritual priority over the material world. If this is unclear to you, consider what Jesus said about serving two masters; it can't be done, you cannot serve God and mammon (Matthew 6:24). At the same time, we must acknowledge that being rich does not constitute being outside the will of God.

Abraham, Joseph, Job, and Solomon were all men of great wealth. Jesus had followers who were wealthy, and no doubt there are many Christian men and women today who are wealthy. It's not evil to be wealthy. It becomes evil when you think you need wealth to experience what it means to be a Christian.

If you are wealthy, know that God hasn't given you wealth as an end in itself. Most likely, He has given you wealth so that you can give to those who are needy. In the midst of this, your needs and the needs of others are being met, and through it, God is being glorified. When the message of the gospel is reduced to wealth being the primary characteristic and validation of what it means to be a Christian, that message proves to be inconsistent worldwide.

If it all comes down to the right kind of faith, the right kind of praying, and sowing your money into the right kind of prosperity ministry, then we should all have a Mercedes Benz parked in our front yard. Christians living in Third World countries should be able to have the same results praying for wealth as do Christians praying for wealth in North America. If it all comes down to a matter of faith and positive confession, we should all have the same material things throughout the world wherever Christians are full of faith and practice positive confession. If the principles and results of God's truth are not the same worldwide, then it must not be His truth, for His truth works in every part and corner of the world.

What we have done in North America is to make Christianity synonymous with the American dream. Christ knew nothing about an American dream. His dream was about making disciples of all nations. That's the purpose of the Great Commission. It is taking the truth of redemption to the whole world, where everyone experiences

God's forgiveness, a reconnecting with God, and the unfolding of redemption in their lives.

Is the American dream wrong? Hard work, honesty, and integrity in all of life's transactions are characteristics that can count on God's blessings. However, if the American dream becomes the only thing you live for, then the American dream really becomes the American idol for idol worshipers.

> Do not love the world or the things in the world. If anyone loves the world, the love of the Father is not in him. For all that is in the world—the lust of the flesh, the lust of the eyes, and the pride of life—is not of the Father but is of the world. And the world is passing away, and the lust of it; but he who does the will of God abides forever. 1 John 2:15–17

Competition In the Body of Christ

God's calling on your life doesn't mean the goal is to be the pastor of the largest church, the best preacher, the best teacher, or the best contemporary Christian artist. There is nothing wrong with the desire to do the best you can and to continue developing the raw talent and abilities God has gifted you with. You should desire to do your best for God. However, your best for God should never be measured by how well you compare with others.

In the parable of the talents in Matthew 25, the man traveling to a far country called his servants and gave them his goods. Notice that the goods never originated from the servants. They were always the master's goods. When the master returned, he found that only two of the three servants had been faithfully working with what had been given to them. When the master rewarded them, he did not reward them on the basis of how well they had competed with one another. He rewarded them on the basis of their faithfulness to what each one had been given to do, making competition and comparison a nonissue in the family of God.

God rewards you on the basis of your obedience, not your talent. The talent or giftedness was not yours in the first place. That was given to you, or better yet, loaned to you, it was always His from the beginning. How can God reward you on the basis of talent or giftedness that was His from the start? He can reward you only on the basis of what you did with what He gave you. The abilities, talents, and spiritual gifts God has placed in your life are ways for you to know what His purpose is for your life.

You have the calling of using what He gave you to bring glory and honor to His name. When you highlight who God is through your calling, everyone wins, because the greatest need humans have is to see the goodness of God in a broken, hurting world.

> Let your light so shine before men, that they may see
> your good works and glorify your Father in heaven.
> Matthew 5:16

There is no place for arrogance or prideful feelings in which Christians feel they are above others. Everything belongs to God, even the breath we breathe. To be active in your calling is not some competitive race in which you are competing with other Christians. You are not in competition with anyone but yourself. No one else can do what God has called you to do, only you can. Paul reminded the competitive church in Corinth that it is not about the one who plants or the one who waters, but God who is able to give the increase (1

Corinthians 3:7). Nevertheless, to the one who has been called to plant or to water, there is no greater fulfillment in life than to be doing these things.

Is Calling Always Done Inside The Four Walls of the Church?

It is not uncommon to think that calling is limited to what we are accustomed to seeing in the context of a church building, such as pastors, worship leaders, Sunday school teachers, elders, and deacons. God's calling however is not restricted to only the things we do inside the church building or on the mission field. God's calling is both internal and external. Internally is what we do through the ministries of the church. This is our kingdom building. It involves life training so that we can be the salt and light disciples of Christ to the world. Externally is what we do in kingdom expanding. It is taking the gospel to the marketplace where people live, work, and play. Jesus said that we are the salt and light of the world, not the salt and light of the church to be kept inside a building.

Often what we do as a church body—and not intentionally, I believe, but ignorantly—is to keep ministry confined to the four walls of a church building. Being the salt and light of the world means that in order to be seen, we have to go where people live, work, and play. The Great Commission is to go out and make disciples of all nations. In many of our evangelical churches, what we have in place is a "come and get it" evangelism. If you want Christ, come to church on Sunday.

Perhaps we should learn from Jesus, who applied an all-encompassing strategy when preaching the good news of the gospel. He did not limit preaching the good news to synagogues. Obviously, He used traditional methods that were in place in His day, but He also used nontraditional methods. His first life seminar was not held in the

Jerusalem convention center, but on a hillside. He literally took the good news of the gospel to where people lived.

Perhaps you have never considered your professional career as an extension of God's kingdom purpose on earth. Maybe it's time we should consider the secular world of work the new missionary field for the work of the gospel. For Christians who live out their Christianity 24-7, the work place provides a new missionary field for the gospel of love to be seen in action. I believe this is what Jesus had in mind when He called us the salt and light of the world (Matthew 5:13-14).

If you are a Christian, know that you are bringing a sample of what happened on church Sunday morning to people who were not in church but who nevertheless still need salt and light exposure. Through you and the work you do, whether you are a doctor, a librarian, or a construction worker, you become the point of contact for other people who are in your line of work to see how the gospel works in everyday real life situations. Obviously we are not going to force the gospel upon anyone, but the character fruit of the Holy Spirit cannot go unnoticed in darken places.

> But sanctify the Lord God in your hearts, and always
> *be* ready to *give* a defense to everyone who asks you
> a reason for the hope that is in you, with meekness
> and fear   1 Peter 3:15

It is in the marketplace, especially in the culture that we live in today, where the need is the greatest to see how God's redemption works in real life situations. Perhaps the reason for the growing decay in society today is that the body of Christ insists on keeping the light and salt within the four walls of the church building, instead of in the world where it is needed most.

What Your Calling Means in Everyday Life

It is important to understand that God's purpose is the key to your personal life fulfillment. Too often fulfillment in life eludes us because as Myles Monroe says in *Releasing Your Potential:* "we look everywhere but God for the meaning of our existence."[12] God created everything with a specific purpose in mind. In highlighting God's ordered design and purpose the psalmist wrote this concerning nature:

He sends the springs into the valleys;
They flow among the hills.
They give drink to every beast of the field;
The wild donkeys quench their thirst.
By them the birds of the heavens have their home;
They sing among the branches.
He waters the hills from His upper chambers;
The earth is satisfied with the fruit of Your works.
He causes the grass to grow for the cattle,
And vegetation for the service of man,
That he may bring forth food from the earth,
And wine that makes glad the heart of man,
Oil to make his face shine,
And bread which strengthens man's heart.
The trees of the LORD are full of sap,
The cedars of Lebanon which He planted,
Where the birds make their nests;
The stork has her home in the fir trees.
The high hills are for the wild goats;
The cliffs are a refuge for the rock badgers.
He appointed the moon for seasons;

The sun knows its going down.

You make darkness, and it is night,

In which all the beasts of the forest creep about.

The young lions roar after their prey,

And seek their food from God.

When the sun rises, they gather together

And lie down in their dens.

Man goes out to his work

And to his labor until the evening.

O Lord, how manifold are Your works!

In wisdom You have made them all.

The earth is full of Your possessions.

Psalm 104:10–24

It is difficult to deny the architectural wisdom and sovereignty of God. The same order, design, and purpose are true in the life of every human being. In Psalm 139, David wrote:

O Lord, You have searched me and known me.

You know my sitting down and my rising up;

You understand my thought afar off.

You comprehend my path and my lying down,

And are acquainted with all my ways.

For there is not a word on my tongue,

But behold, O Lord, You know it altogether.

You have hedged me behind and before,

And laid Your hand upon me.

Such knowledge is too wonderful for me;

It is high, I cannot attain it.

Where can I go from Your Spirit?

Or where can I flee from Your presence?

If I ascend into heaven, You are there;

If I make my bed in hell, behold, You are there.

If I take the wings of the morning,

And dwell in the uttermost parts of the sea,

Even there Your hand shall lead me,

And Your right hand shall hold me.

If I say, "Surely the darkness shall fall on me,"

Even the night shall be light about me;

Indeed, the darkness shall not hide from You,

But the night shines as the day;

The darkness and the light are both alike to You.

For You formed my inward parts;

You covered me in my mother's womb.

I will praise You, for I am fearfully and

Wonderfully made; Marvelous are Your works,

And that my soul knows very well.

My frame was not hidden from You,

When I was made in secret,

And skillfully wrought in the lowest parts of the earth.

Your eyes saw my substance, being yet unformed.

And in Your book they all were written,

The days fashioned for me,

When as yet there were none of them.

Psalm 139:1–16

God is not only active in His creation as it relates to nature, He was also active in bringing the realization of your birth into this world. You are not an accident nor are you a mistake, nor are you unwanted and without significance. You are the very reason why Christ died and rose from the dead.

Redemption: God's Will for Your Life

> He has delivered us from the power of darkness and
> conveyed us into the kingdom of the Son of His love,
> in whom we have redemption through His blood, the
> forgiveness of sins.   Colossians 1:13–14

So what is God's will and plan for your life? Through the work of Jesus Christ, you have been called to live in a meaningful process of redemption and restoration that begins with a reconnecting with God. That is the meaning of the cross of Jesus Christ. It is your reconnecting point with God that unfolds in life's greatest acceptance (*justification*), life's greatest character growth (*sanctification*), life's greatest purpose (*calling*), ending in life's greatest destiny (*glorification*).

Redemption involves your complete whole life not just parts of it. It involves changing the way you think about yourself. As such, it impacts your self-esteem and your self-concept. You live out of a new identity that allows you the greatest freedom and expression of life, not the fear and the self-doubt that grow from the experiences of a fallen world. Redemption is about God's Holy Spirit empowering your life with the character of God that makes you both beautiful and strong.

Redemption is about becoming an extension of God's kingdom purpose which allows you the greatest life adventure, a life lived with meaning and purpose that exceeds the duration of life. Redemption's ultimate purpose is to remove you completely from the fallen world and the presence of sin into the presence of God. Through Jesus Christ, God has destined you to be His child, to live under the authority and character of His name. Your greatest potential in life will never result from living separately from Him.

God did not create you with the desires and giftedness He put in you to be placed on a shelf. You are His showcase to the world of His awesome workmanship and power to redeem from the brokenness of a fallen world. He desires for you to use and develop what He has given you, to honor Him as your heavenly Father who is full of mercy, full of grace, and who believes and supports your greatest life adventure.

Chapter 7

Life's Greatest Keeping
(How God Keeps Us)

Earlier the point was made that there can be no greater destiny unfolding in the lives of humans than God working through Jesus Christ to redeem broken humanity. Nothing in life can be compared to our reconnecting with God. It is truly the greatest human comeback story in the history of the most unlikely champions in life. However, as the process of redemption comes to its conclusion, we must remember that redemption is not only about the incredible journey God walks us through in life. The ultimate purpose of redemption is to be eternally reunited with God in His home. Heaven is the eternal destination and reward of the redeemed. All those God has accepted as His sons and daughters through Christ are citizens of heaven. Jesus made this point very clear when the disciples returned rejoicing from a short missionary trip.

> Then the seventy returned with joy, saying, "Lord, even the demons are subject to us in Your name." And He said to them, "I saw Satan fall like lightning from heaven. Behold, I give you the authority to trample

> on serpents and scorpions, and over all the power of
> the enemy, and nothing shall by any means hurt you.
> Nevertheless do not rejoice in this, that the spirits are
> subject to you, but rather rejoice because your names
> are written in heaven."   Luke 10:17-20

In the final part of God's redemptive process the concern now turns to the assurance of arriving at our final destination. What a tragedy it would be to have been in the process of redemption your whole life but in the end not make the trip home. As contradictory as this is in light of the fact that God redeems sinners on the basis of what Christ has accomplished and not human merit, it is here that disagreement exists in the body of Christ. Some believe that salvation can be lost. In the end, some of the redeemed will not make it to the redemption celebration banquet in heaven. This leads us to question the power the atonement of Jesus Christ has over the effects of sin.

Recalculating the Power of Christ to Save from Sin

If it is true that salvation can be lost we must then ask, on what basis? If it is lost on the basis of sin, then obviously the power in the blood of the Lamb who takes away the sin of the world must be recalculated (John 1:29). Either the sacrifice of Jesus was fully sufficient to redeem completely from the penalty of sin, or sin indeed has the power to actually dilute and diminish the efficacy of Christ's sacrifice. If this is the case, then clearly we must add personal effort to the sacrifice of Christ. However, the need to add personal effort to our salvation makes us co-redeemers with Christ in our own salvation. This clearly contradicts Scripture in addition to being blasphemous.

> For by grace you have been saved through faith, and
> that not of yourselves; it is the gift of God, not of
> works, lest anyone should boast.   Ephesians 2:8–9

If salvation can be lost as a result of sinful behavior, then there are at least three questions that need clear and direct answers from the Bible.

How Much Sin Is Too Much?

This is a critical question that every Christian needs to know for obvious reasons. What does the Bible say about how many times a particular sin or sins can be committed before one has crossed the point of no return? What is the number of sins? We really need to have this information locked down, don't you think? Those who believe you can lose your salvation usually don't have any clue as to how much sin would result in this tragedy.

The New Testament never gives us any idea or clue as to how many sins are too many. Additionally, if Christ died for all the sins of the world—past, present, and future—how is it that some sins were not covered by His sacrifice? If it is true that sin is the basis for losing salvation, then realistically we must all be in jeopardy of losing it, if we haven't lost it already.

The reason being is that since the time of our conversion, no one, in an absolute sense has become sin free, nor has anyone reached a maturity in life beyond the point of being tempted and falling into sin. Obviously this is our battle with the flesh as we strive to fight the good fight and not fall or give in to anything that is against God's character. However, anyone claiming to be flawless on this side of heaven is just in complete utter denial. In Philippians 3:12, Paul himself said that he had not reached sinless perfection.

Who Determines How Much Is Too Much?

This question is equally important because here again it is obvious that human beings are not the standard by which God gives grace or withholds grace. Who then decides the point of no return? One thing I know for sure, you and I don't determine what the point of no return is for anyone. Paul gives us this assurance in writing to the Christians at Rome.

> What then shall we say to these things? If God is for us, who can be against us? He who did not spare His own Son, but delivered Him up for us all, how shall He not with Him also freely give us all things? Who shall bring a charge against God's elect? It is God who justifies. Who is he who condemns? It is Christ who died, and furthermore is also risen, who is even at the right hand of God, who also makes intercession for us.
>
> Romans 8:31–34

How Do Christians Who Believe You Can Lose Your Salvation Continue to Remain Saved?

Since there are no Christians who can honestly say they have reached a sinless maturity in life, how do they remain saved? Are there sins we can commit that don't result in losing salvation and other sins that automatically result in losing salvation? Who determines what is on the list of sins that can be committed and still remain okay with God versus sins committed in which God declares He is through with us?

Since there is no biblical list given to us on this subject, here's how it commonly works among people who believe you can lose your salvation. When people sin, for those who claim to remain saved, grace rises in proportion to their sin, therefore leaving them still in good standing with God.

The problem with this particular way of dealing with personal sin, as we have already noted; is that believers are not the standard for measuring the extent of grace. At best, this kind of reasoning has no place to land except on hypocrisy. When judging others, we often judge them on their behavior, but when we judge ourselves, we judge by our motives. Judgment by motives is always less harsh than judgment by behavior.

The logical conclusion to believing you can lose your salvation becomes problematic for every Christian. Reason being is that no believer reaches, nor will we ever reach sinless perfection on this side of heaven. If you think you are sinless, your understanding of God's holiness is extremely limited and unrealistic. On the other hand, if it is determined that sin is what causes one to lose salvation, what is the difference between Christians who sin and yet remain saved and Christians who sin and lose their salvation?

We Need a Clear Definition of What It Means to be Saved

Perhaps what is needed in resolving this issue is a clear understanding of what it means to really be saved. Jesus gave us a clear, indisputable definition of what it means to be saved and heaven bound in the Gospel of John.

> Jesus answered and said to him, "Most assuredly, I
> say to you, unless one is born again, he cannot see the

kingdom of God." Nicodemus said to Him, "How can
a man be born when he is old? Can he enter a second
time into his mother's womb and be born?" Jesus
answered, "Most assuredly, I say to you, unless one
is born of water and the Spirit, he cannot enter the
kingdom of God."   John 3:3–5

For Jesus, the defining mark of what it means to be a true
Christian whose part is in the kingdom of God, is to be born again.
This definition brings some clarity to what we have often mistaken
as evidence of salvation.

Being in the Fellowship of Believers Does Not Make One Born Again

Judas was one of the twelve disciples of Jesus Christ who was
privileged to take part in His ministry. For three years; he lived and
walked with Jesus, he heard all the teaching of Jesus and saw all the
miracles Jesus did. In fact, he himself would have participated in the
preaching, healing, and the casting out of demons according to the
Gospel of Mark.

And He called the twelve to Himself, and began to
send them out two by two, and gave them power over
unclean spirits. He commanded them to take nothing
for the journey except a staff—no bag, no bread, no
copper in their money belts—but to wear sandals, and
not to put on two tunics. Also He said to them, "In
whatever place you enter a house, stay there till you
depart from that place. And whoever will not receive
you nor hear you, when you depart from there, shake
off the dust under your feet as a testimony against

> them. Assuredly, I say to you, it will be more toler-
> able for Sodom and Gomorrah in the day of judgment
> than for that city!" So they went out and preached that
> people should repent.   Mark 6:7–12

Judas's life could stand as a good argument for the case of losing your salvation; after all, he was involved with Jesus from the beginning of His ministry to the end. The real issue concerning the life of Judas is not that he was numbered as one of the twelve disciples, the real concern is was he truly born again?

The Son of Perdition

In the Gospel of John, the evangelist wrote that no one needed to tell Jesus what was in the heart of man. All men and women are equally exposed before Christ. No one can hide his true heart from God, He sees and understands our deepest secrets (John 2:25). In Jesus' priestly prayer recorded in John 17, He prayed this:

> While I was with them in the world, I kept them in
> Your name. Those whom You gave Me I have kept;
> and none of them is lost except the son of perdition,
> that the Scripture might be fulfilled.   John 17:12

When Jesus made reference to Judas, He called him "the son of perdition." This title given to Judas came from Jesus who knows the whole truth about what lies deep in the heart of every man and woman. What did Jesus know about Judas that was hidden from the other disciples? He knew he was the son of perdition. When did Judas become the son of perdition? Was it when Jesus calmed the storm on the sea and they all wondered who He was that even the wind and the sea obeyed Him (Mark 4:41)?

Was it when Jesus raised Lazarus from the tomb after he had been dead four days (John 11:39)? Was it at the very moment that Jesus called him the son of perdition? No, the answer is, Judas had been the son of perdition from the very beginning. Judas had never been born again in spite of the fact that he had lived with the One who gave the new birth. Being called the son of perdition clues us in to the nature of Judas' heart. In 2 Thessalonians, Paul wrote to encourage the Christian community regarding the coming of the Lord, he said:

> Let no one deceive you by any means; for that Day will not come unless the falling away comes first, and the man of sin is revealed, the son of perdition, who opposes and exalts himself above all that is called God or that is worshiped, so that he sits as God in the temple of God, showing himself that he is God.
>
> 2 Thessalonians 2:3–4

From these verses in 2 Thessalonians chapter 2, we can clearly see that the nature identified with the son of perdition has very little to do with being born again. Foremost, the title *son of perdition* that was given to Judas is the same title given to the Antichrist. The character that was revealed in Judas will be the same character revealed in the Antichrist. Judas may have walked and lived with Jesus, but when Jesus exposes him as the son of perdition, we immediately know he was never one of God's children. Judas was not one who was saved but then through a series of bad choices lost his salvation. It is not uncommon for us to feel a sense of great loss in what Judas did in betraying Jesus and in what he did to himself. After all, he was one of the so-called disciples. However, behind the scenes of what appeared to be real, we must remember that according to Jesus Himself, Judas had always been the son of perdition and not the son of a born again experience.

Being Religious Doesn't Make One Born Again (Scribes and Pharisees)

During the time of Jesus' earthly ministry, there were two religious groups that were key components to the religious system of that day. The scribes were responsible for copying the laws of God and eventually were thought to be the authoritative interpreters of the law of God. On the other hand, the Pharisees were extremely zealous for obeying the laws of God, maintaining their personal holiness before God and for their man-made traditions. Through the Gospels we know that these men occupied a very high and respectful place in the eyes of the people. They played a very significant role in the spiritual development of those who trusted in their guidance. Nevertheless, it was these religious groups that Jesus exposed as not being real.

In Matthew 23, Jesus denounced the scribes and the Pharisees, calling them hypocrites, sons of hell, whitewashed tombs, lawless, serpents, and a brood of vipers. In the context of being born again, the identifying mark of what it means to be saved, chapter 23 of Matthew stands out as what it means to *not* be born again. In Matthew 5, Jesus revealed the truth about the spiritual reality of the Pharisees which surely must have shocked His listeners.

> For I say to you, that unless your righteousness
> exceeds the righteousness of the scribes and Pharisees,
> you will by no means enter the kingdom of heaven.
> Matthew 5:20

In reviewing the case of the scribes and Pharisees, as well as the life of Judas. Being religious leaders in the community or being in the fellowship of Christ's disciples; did not necessarily mean they were in an authentic salvation experience. Salvation can only be validated by the experience of being born again which manifests itself through bearing the fruit of the Spirit. With regard to the scribes and the Pharisees, these were not people who had been saved and then lost their salvation.

What Jesus revealed about them was that they had never been born again. Perhaps you have seen this scenario once or twice in your lifetime. A person you know may have been very active in church maybe even held a position in the church. Suddenly and without warning, this person returns to living the life of an unsaved person. It would appear to all who knew this person that he or she had been really saved, but the question remains, were they born again?

The Parable of the Sower

The parable of the sower in Matthew 13 provides some guidance for us with regards to who is truly born again. In this parable, Jesus described four responses to the gospel which still hold true today. Truly born again people endure the tests of trials and the lures of a fallen world, and as the parable indicates bear fruit.

Wayside Responders

Jesus said that the seed the birds devoured by the wayside are those who hear the message but don't understand it. The lack of understanding creates a strong barrier that doesn't allow them to commit to the gospel. Both the Lord Jesus and the apostle Paul agreed that behind the scenes, Satan is working to extinguish faith in God.

> But even if our gospel is veiled, it is veiled to those
> who are perishing, whose minds the god of this age

has blinded, who do not believe, lest the light of the
gospel of the glory of Christ, who is the image of God,
should shine on them.   2 Corinthian 4:3–4

Many people have difficulty harmonizing the God of love and power with a world of injustice and suffering, and therefore cannot believe in the God of the Bible. People such as these never live beyond what they can validate through their five senses. If they can't see it, they don't believe it. The option for the supernatural is closed to them, even though it is evil supernatural forces that are working in them to destroy their faith.

Stony Ground Responders

Concerning the seed that fell among the stony ground, Jesus said these were people who immediately received the Word with joy, yet they had no root in themselves. The fact that they had no root in themselves describes only an emotional response to the gospel. For the gospel to be rooted in us, it requires not only an emotional response, but also an intellectual assent. The reason being is that in due time, the heart will always follow the mind. Young children can easily be convinced in their innocent hearts of the tooth fairy or of Santa Claus, but it would be difficult to find a teenager or a forty-year-old man still believing in Santa Claus. Why we lie to our sons and daughters giving them hope in something that is not real is beyond me. What's wrong with the truth? Nevertheless, those on the stony ground do appear to be real believers. However, faith that does not exceed an emotional response cannot survive the assaults of a broken world.

Thorny Ground Responders

The thorny ground responders are those whose hearts have not been changed by the new birth. They apparently wanted the message of the gospel, but not at the cost of giving up the pursuits of the world. To them, the cares of this life and the deceitfulness of riches turn out to be the better pursuit in life. Bearing the fruit of the Holy Spirit is the clear evidence of being born again. Jesus Himself said these thorny-ground responders were not fruitful.

Good Ground Responders

The good ground responders are those who hear the Word, and in contrast to the first responders who didn't understand it, they understand it perhaps not perfectly, but nevertheless find refuge in it as the foundation for life. Additionally, because the Word brings meaning and hope to life, they are able to endure beyond the assaults of a broken world. In contrast to those who ultimately show allegiance to the pursuit of things, they with patience bear the fruit of being in an authentic relationship with God.

The Parable of the Good Shepherd

In the parable of the good shepherd, Jesus said He knew the sheep that were His and His sheep knew Him. The word *know* in this context conveys the idea of knowing intimately through experience. Jesus elaborated the meaning of this word *know* by saying that He knows His sheep in the same way the Father knows Him, the point is clear— intimate knowledge.

> I am the good shepherd; and I know My own sheep,
> and am know by My own. As the Father knows Me,

147

> even so I know the Father; and I lay down My life for
> the sheep. John 10:14-15

This relationship results in His sheep hearing His voice and following Him. Additionally, Jesus said that He gives them eternal life, and no one is able to pluck them out of His hands. The reason for this eternal security is that the Father who gave them to Him is greater than all (John 10:27–30).

> And I give them eternal life, and they will never
> perish; neither shall anyone one snatch them out of
> My hand. My Father, who has given them to Me, is
> greater than all; and no one is able to snatch them out
> of My Father's hand. John 10:28–29

The Parable of the Ten Virgins

In the parable of the ten virgins, it is not necessary to look at all the particulars because Jesus Himself gives us the conclusive answer to the question of authentic salvation in verse 12.

> Afterward the other virgins came also, saying,
> "Lord, Lord, open to us!" But he answered and said,
> "Assuredly, I say to you, I do not know you."
> Matthew 25:11–12

The passage we just saw where Jesus declared He knew His sheep intimately sheds important light on the passage we are now considering. Jesus did not say, He once knew the five virgins; He simply responded saying that He did not know them. Could Jesus have known the five foolish virgins at one time and then deny He ever knew them? Wouldn't this make Jesus a lair? There is no room for speculation in the words *I do not know you*. Perhaps the problem with the parable of the ten virgins is in looking too hard at all the details in the story and not giving final authority to the words Jesus Himself declared. This brings to mind Matthew chapter 7.

> "Not everyone who says to Me, 'Lord, Lord,' shall enter the kingdom of heaven, but he who does the will of My Father in heaven. Many will say to Me in that day, 'Lord, Lord, have we not prophesied in Your name, cast out demons in Your name, and done many wonders in Your name?' And then I will declare to them, 'I never knew you; depart from Me, you who practice lawlessness!' Matthew 7:21–23

To those who apparently were giving great manifestations of the anointing of God through mighty works of miracles, it may surprise us to hear Jesus say, "I never knew you; depart from Me," Jesus did not say, "I knew you once, and then I stopped knowing you." His clear words are "I never knew you." Obviously these are not believers who will lose their salvation in the end, these are professing men who were never in a born again salvation experience with the Lord Jesus Christ.

The Parable of the Talents (Matthew 25:14)

In the parable of the talents, the man who went on the journey obviously represents Christ, and the servants represent professing believers. From what we have already learned from the example of Judas; who was *among* the fellowship of believers but not *in* an authentic relationship with the Savior, to the scribes and Pharisees,— these examples all shed light on the parable of the talents. The parable suggests that all who are in true relationship with God will bear fruit to some degree. Fruit bearing is the evidence of salvation, as we saw in the parable of the sower in which those who were the good-ground responders bore fruit, some thirtyfold, some sixtyfold, and some a hundredfold. All who are in true relationship with God will bear fruit.

In the parable of the talents, it must be noted that failure to be successful upon the master's return was not due to the hardness of the master. Each one was assigned a task according to his ability to work. One servant was given five talents; to another two talents, the last servant was given only one talent. Failure would not be based on the unreasonable demands of the master, but only by the lack of response to the grace each one had been given. They were all given grace through the talents that would render them profitable servants upon the master's return.

The task was easy and fair and would be extremely rewarding upon the return of the master, but only two accepted the privilege of grace that had been given to them. When the master returned to settle accounts the last servant proved to be completely indifferent towards the grace that had been given to him. He had done absolutely nothing, not even the minimal. In fact, the only thing he did was to give excuses for rejecting his master's grace. From the argument of Jesus, that only the born again are truly His, it would be extremely difficult to make the case that the servant with the one talent was really in an authentic relationship with the master.

He too had been invited to participate in the master's grace, but he refused to respond in a way that demonstrated he had accepted the conditions. Listen to his responses upon the master's return:

1. "I knew you to be a hard man . . ." (Matthew 25:24).

It would be impossible to find any Christian on this planet under the grace of God who would address God in this manner.

2. " . . . reaping where you have not sown, and gathering where you have not scattered seed" (Matthew 25:24).

Again, among the believers in the whole wide world, would we find a born again child of God who would challenge God's sovereignty as this servant did?

3. "I was afraid" (Matthew 25:25).

Those who have understood the grace and mercy of God's goodness do not respond to a relationship with God with fear, but with an attitude of worship.

4. "I . . . hid your talent in the ground. Look, there you have what is yours" (Matthew 25:25).

In the end, this servant never took ownership of his master's gift of grace. He rejected it and gave back the grace that had been offered to him.

5. "You wicked and lazy servant . . ." (Matthew 25:26).

In the end, *wicked and lazy servant* are not terms related to the fruits of repentance. James said that authentic faith is always accompanied by works—not that works save us, but works are the evidence of salvation.

> Thus also faith by itself, if it does not have works, is dead. But someone will say, "You have faith, and I have works." Show me your faith without your works,

and I will show you my faith by my works.

James 2:17–18

In the end, it is extremely difficult to come to a conclusion that the servant described in the parable as wicked and lazy could have been a believer who had lost his salvation. What is clear in the parable is that the last servant never took ownership of what had been offered to him. But what is the purpose of the warnings in these parables if they do not imply the obvious? You are right—these parables do serve as warnings, but not to born again believers. First, they serve as warnings not to reject the grace of God that is offered to us through Jesus Christ, and second they serve as warnings to those who claim to be in a relationship with God but that are not bearing the fruit of a born again experience.

Knowledge of the Truth Doesn't Make One Born Again

Knowledge of the truth does not make one born again. A case in point would be demons. James said that even demons "believe and tremble" (James 2:19). Additionally, demons recognized who Jesus was before any of the religious leaders did. In fact, not only did the religious leaders not recognize Jesus, but they were the primary planners in His crucifixion. Here are a few things that may surprise you that demons can do. In Mark chapter 1, when Jesus was teaching in Capernaum they were among the first to recognize who Jesus was.

> Now there was a man in their synagogue with an unclean spirit. And he cried out, saying, "Let us alone! What have we to do with You, Jesus of Nazareth? Did You come to destroy us? I know who You are—the Holy One of God!" Mark 1:23–24

152

In Mark 5, when Jesus and His disciples came to the region of the Gadarenes, demons worshiped Him and actually uttered a prayer of desperation.

> When he saw Jesus from afar, he ran and worshiped Him. And he cried out with a loud voice and said, "What have I to do with You, Jesus, Son of the Most High God? I implore You by God that You do not torment me." Mark 5:6–7

From the book of Acts, we also know that demons can possess people and actually proclaim truth.

> Now it happened, as we went to prayer, that a certain slave girl possessed with a spirit of divination met us, who brought her masters much profit by fortune-telling. This girl followed Paul and us, and cried out, saying, "These men are the servants of the Most High God, who proclaim to us the way of salvation." And this she did for many days. But Paul, greatly annoyed, turned and said to the spirit, "I command you in the name of Jesus Christ to come out of her." And he came out that very hour. Acts 16:16–18

The False Prophets of the Last Days

The fact that Jesus said in the last days there would be many false teachers demands that we carefully examine the fruit bearing of salvation of all who claim to be the prophets of God.

> Beware of false prophets, who come to you in sheep's clothing, but inwardly they are ravenous wolves. You

> will know them by their fruits. Do men gather grapes from thorn bushes or figs from thistles? Even so, every good tree bears good fruit, but a bad tree bears bad fruit. A good tree cannot bear bad fruit, nor can a bad tree bear good fruit. Every tree that does not bear good fruit is cut down and thrown into the fire. Therefore by their fruits you will know them.   Matthew 7:15–20

The things Jesus said about false prophets are extremely alarming for two main reasons. First, we cannot detect them simply by appearance. In appearance they look authentic, harmless, and sincere about helping us in our spiritual development. Second, from that Jesus said earlier in Matthew 7:21 they possess powers that people normally would identify as men with special anointing from God. Note the lure of false prophets. They appear harmless in character and powerful in works. What else could we want from our spiritual leaders besides humility and powerful anointing? However, Jesus said that not all who cast out demons and do wonders are in a born again relationship with Him. In fact, He said that on that day, many will say, "Have we not prophesied in Your name? Have we not delivered people from Satan's hand? Have we not demonstrated Your power through wonders?" (see Matthew 7:22). Jesus will respond by saying, "I never knew you; depart from Me, you who practice lawlessness" (Matthew 7:23).

What Lawlessness Looks Like?

The apostle Peter gives us clear characteristics of what lawlessness looks like in chapter 2 of his second epistle.

1. Lawlessness denies the deity of Christ.

Denying the Lord Jesus is denying the only means by which a person through faith can enter into a relationship with God. Without Christ, there is no forgiveness of sin nor salvation for any of us (2 Peter 2:1).

2. Lawlessness seeks covetousness as the only aim in life.

False prophets know something about what is in human nature and exploit it to the fullest extent by offering individuals what they know they want, and then by putting a price on it for their own benefit. Peter says that these false teachers present great swelling messages and grandiose teaching that have the power to mesmerize those who have the appetite for grandiose lifestyles. Peter says that the reason grandiose preaching works is because people have grandiose lifestyles in their hearts (2 Peter 2:12, 18). For those whose desire in life is bent towards materialism, materialistic preaching is what they will respond to. This kind of teaching, however, attempts to make God into our image rather than have us grow in His image. The first false teacher of the grandiose lifestyle was Satan himself, when he promised Adam and Eve that they themselves could be like God (Genesis 3:5).

3. Lawlessness has no desire to repent.

False prophets will not accept correction because they operate out of their own truth. As such, they will always claim to have a higher revelation than what is given to all of us through the Scriptures. They will resist any rebuke that calls for repentance, which is the first step towards a genuine relationship with God. Peter compared the false prophets to the angels who rebelled along with Satan, to the people of Noah's day, and to the cites of Sodom and Gomorrah. What did all these individuals have in common? No desire to repent and make things right with God (2 Peter 2:4–7).

4. Lawlessness lives to pleasure the flesh.

Peter described false prophets as walking in the flesh and despising authority. They are self-willed people who live only to please and pleasure themselves. For this reason, Peter compared them to natural brute beasts. Several things can be noted about animals. First, they do not reason and think through the consequences of their behavior. Second, they live only to satisfy their instincts. Third, to assure their own survival they prey on animals that are weaker than they are. Fourth, they have no knowledge of being caught and destroyed. There can be no sadder description of human beings created in the image of God than those who refuse the grace and mercy of God.

Does 2 Peter Chapter 2 Depict Believers Who Were Once Saved But Lost Their Salvation?

> For if, after they have escaped the pollutions of the world through the knowledge of the Lord and Savior Jesus Christ, they are again entangled in them and overcome, the latter end is worse for them than the beginning. For it would have been better for them not to have known the way of righteousness, than having known it, to turn from the holy commandment delivered to them. But it has happened to them according to the true proverb: "A dog returns to his own vomit," and, "a sow, having washed, to her wallowing in the mire."
> 2 Peter 2:20–22

For the most part, 2 Peter chapter 2 is revealing the characteristics of *false teachers* not the characteristics of being born again. This is indisputable from verse 1 in chapter 2. The false teachers are those who will "secretly bring destructive heresies, even denying the Lord" (2 Peter 2:1). They cannot be considered Christians with a genuine born again experience. A *second group* is mentioned in verse 2; these are the followers of the false teachers; "And many will follow their destructive ways." They also cannot be considered born again Christians since they are following the false teachers.

A *third group* could be those mentioned in verse 18 which Peter says the false teachers allured through the lusts of the flesh.

> For when they speak great swelling words of emptiness, they allure through the lusts of the flesh, through lewdness, the ones who have actually escaped from those who live in error.   2 Peter 2:18

From Peter's testimony it is obvious that these individuals whom he said had escaped, did not escape for a very long time. They were lured back through the swelling empty words of the false prophets and by the lusts of the flesh. This parallels the parable Jesus spoke regarding the seed that was sowed among the thorns. They received the seed of the gospel, but the cares and the deceitfulness of riches made the seed unfruitful. In the midst of chapter 2 there is this wonderful promise in verse 9, which says the following:

> The Lord knows how to deliver the godly out of temptations and to reserve the unjust under punishment for the day of judgment.   2 Peter 2:9

The critical question here has to do with the provision in verse 9. Why weren't the individuals mentioned in verse 18 covered by the promise of verse 9? Did God forget to deliver them from temptation? Isn't this the promise of verse 9? "The Lord knows how to deliver the godly out of temptations." Then why were they not delivered? The answer is that they apparently were not God's very own. Later, the fact that they were not God's own through a genuine born again experience is validated by what Peter said in verse 22.

> But it has happened to them according to the true proverb: "A dog returns to his own vomit," and, "a sow, having washed, to her wallowing in the mire."
>
> 2 Peter 2:22

Verse 22 is the key to understanding the issue at hand. Their nature had not yet been transformed by the new nature that comes from a genuine born again experience; as such, they returned to do what was in their very own nature. Change that is man-made will be only temporary, while born again change that is through the Holy Spirit lasts forever.

Hebrews 6 Passage

> For it is impossible for those who were once enlightened, and have tasted the heavenly gift, and have become partakers of the Holy Spirit, and have tasted the good word of God and the powers of the age to come, if they fall away, to renew them again to repentance, since they crucify again for themselves the Son of God, and put Him to an open shame.Hebrews 6:4–6

Hebrews chapter 6 verses 4-6 have also been quoted as a reference for the possibility of losing your salvation. It is important to keep in mind the whole context of the book of Hebrews in order to arrive at the best interpretation and avoid an interpretation that rests solely on these verses. As with all interpretation of passages that seem to contradict the clear passages of Scripture, it is always necessary to understand the historical setting in addition to the whole context of the Bible. With regard to what we believe about eternal security, it is necessary to have a clear understanding of how the Old Testament covenant law and New Testament covenant grace interconnect to provide a complete picture of God's salvation.

The Old Testament covenant was clearly based on performance (law keeping), while the New Testament covenant is based on grace (faith keeping). The two covenants cannot coexist in the life of a Christian. Law and grace are incompatible. Law demands justice and punishment, while grace demands mercy and forgiveness. Although they are incompatible with regard to how man stands before God, together they show the complete revelation of God's redemption. The Old Testament covenant is the foundation on which we understand the New Testament, and the New Testament stands as the fulfillment of what was prophesied in the Old Testament. The book of Hebrews makes this exceptionally clear.

From the title of the book, "Hebrews," to the very first chapter and throughout the letter, it is obvious that both the author and the audience to whom the letter was written to were Jewish believers. Gentile believers would have had absolutely no concern for, nor would they have understood the Levitical system of the Old Testament. It is obvious from the onset that the author of Hebrews was writing to reveal the supremacy of Christ over the religious system of the Old Testament.

Therefore, the author of Hebrews begins by saying that in the past, God had always spoken to His covenant people through the prophets, but now He had revealed Himself through Jesus Christ.

> God, who at various times and in various ways spoke in time past to the fathers by the prophets, has in these last days spoken to us by His Son, whom He has appointed heir of all things, through whom also He made the worlds; who being the brightness of His glory and the express image of His person, and upholding all things by the word of His power, when He had by Himself purged our sins, sat down at the right hand of the Majesty on high.   Hebrews 1:1–3

To prove his point, the author of Hebrews goes on to show the supremacy of Christ by revealing that Christ was superior to everything they had trusted in as the basis for God's favor.

Christ is superior to the prophets (chapter 1).

Christ is superior to angels (chapter 1).

Christ is superior to Moses (chapter 3).

Christ is superior to Joshua (chapter 4).

Christ is superior to Aaron (chapter 5).

Christ is superior to the priesthood (chapter 7)

Christ is a superior covenant (chapter 8, verse 7).

The question then is, what was the situation among Jewish believers that the writer of Hebrews felt compelled to show them the supremacy and all-sufficiency of Christ? Four situations occurred in the first century among Jewish believers that necessitated a letter like Hebrews.

(1) Judaism Was Christianity's Rival

Throughout the beginnings of Christianity, Judaism, which was the foundation of Christianity was its greatest rival. As contradictory as this sounds it was indeed the case. Unfortunately for the first-generation Christians, Judaism had more than just one Saul of Tarsus. Judaism had many zealous leaders among its ranks whose love for the Old Testament religious traditions, demanded the suppression and extinction of Christianity wherever it surfaced. In fact, wherever Jewish Christians emerged there was always a countermovement from Jewish religious leaders to bring these erring Jewish converts back to Judaism their true religion.

We see efforts like this in the letter to the Galatians, where obviously the Judaizers had convinced Jewish believers to return to Old Testament law as the basis for right standing with God. Paul responded by reminding the Jewish believers that they had not received the Holy Spirit through the works of the law, but through faith in Jesus Christ.

> This only I want to learn from you: Did you receive the Spirit by the works of the law, or by the hearing of faith? Are you so foolish? Having begun in the Spirit, are you now being made perfect by the flesh?
>
> Galatians 3:2–3

(2) The Persecution of Herod

The second wave of persecution came from the secular leaders of that day. Luke wrote in Acts 12 that Herod the king killed James the brother of John, and when he saw that this pleased the Jews he also had Peter arrested and thrown into prison. Probably the plans were to kill Peter also after the Jewish celebration of the Feast of Unleavened Bread. Jewish Christians found themselves between a rock and a hard place. On one side, they had the Judaizers bombarding Jewish converts making them doubt their newfound faith in Jesus Christ. On the other hand, they had the secular world under the leadership of King Herod killing not only the followers of Christianity, but the very disciples of Christ.

(3) The Jewish Mind-Set

The third element that necessitated a letter like Hebrews was an idea that was deeply ingrained in the mind-set of Judaism. They believed that if they were obedient to God, He would bless them and protect them from their enemies. For this reason, the writer of Hebrews reminded them of the heroes of faith in chapter 11, in order to encourage them not to give up in the midst of hard persecution.

(4) The Leniency of the Roman Government

Add to these circumstances, a fourth variable in which the Roman government had been lenient towards the religion of the Jews, as long as they didn't create an uproar. All these circumstances would have caused even the strongest believers to reevaluate their choice of faith.

The Question of Immorality

It is interesting to note that in the letter to the Hebrews, there is no specific reference to any immorality that could have put their eternal security in jeopardy. In contrast, in the letter written to the Corinthians, there was plenty of immorality going on in the church—immorality that was not even practiced among unbelieving Gentiles—yet Paul never mentioned to them anything about the possibility of losing their salvation. He only said that they should discipline the brother that was practicing immoral acts. However, in Hebrews; there is no mention of any sort of immorality, and yet they are the ones who appear to be in jeopardy. What is going on here? In light of the four historical factors noted, it is clear that the warnings in Hebrews 6 are warnings not to abandon faith in Jesus Christ and return to Judaism as the means for salvation. To return to Judaism would mean the rejection of Jesus Christ. Instead, what they needed to do was to resist the efforts of the Judaizers to bring them back into the religion of their fathers, and remain faithful to Jesus Christ in the midst of severe persecution.

Additionally, what is clear in Hebrews is that the line of denying Jesus and returning to Judaism had not yet been crossed. The word *if* in verse 6 is not describing anyone in particular who had already crossed the line. The reference is purely hypothetical at this point.

However, it is possible that some in the fellowship had become discouraged because of the reasons we just mentioned and may have suggested a return to Judaism. We do know from Hebrews 10:25 that some had stopped gathering with the body of believers. In the immediate context of the letter and in the larger context of the New Testament, this is the best answer to the verse in question. Jewish Christians were having second thoughts about their commitment to

Jesus Christ and contemplating a return to Judaism. In this scenario it makes perfect sense why the author would build a case for the supremacy of Christ. The added warnings are all the more relevant to a situation that had not actually occurred, but one that could occur in the near future without a proper understanding of who Christ was. If this was indeed the case, the author of Hebrews was simply writing out of pastoral concern for those who may have been straddling the fence. One thing is clear however, the situation that led to the writing of this letter had nothing to do with some gross sin or moral failure. It was all about where one stood in reference to believing Christ was the all-sufficient Savior.

The validation of faith in Jesus Christ would not falter in the midst of trials and tribulation. In fact, it would be in the trials that faith would be validated. That is the reason the author assured his audience that there is no salvation in abandoning faith in Christ, and returning to the previous religious system of the Old Testament. The Old Testament covenant was never given to result in redemption; it was given to point to the Christ of the New Testament. The writer of Hebrews however, felt confident that the Jewish believers were remaining strong in the faith.

> But, beloved, we are confident of better things con-
> cerning you, yes, things that accompany salvation,
> though we speak in this manner.   Hebrews 6:9

The Sin unto Death

> If anyone sees his brother sinning a sin which does
> not lead to death, he will ask, and He will give him
> life for those who commit sin not leading to death.
> There is sin leading to death. I do not say that he

should pray about that. All unrighteousness is sin, and there is sin not leading to death. We know that who- ever is born of God does not sin; but he who has been born of God keeps himself, and the wicked one does not touch him.   1 John 5:16–18

The difficulty in this passage comes from what is clearly known from other passages in Scripture. In the passage we are now considering, John appears to classify sin into two categories: sin that does not lead to death and sin that leads to death without resolve. Several factors complicate the idea of putting sin into two categories. First what is clear from the New Testament is that all sin merits death.

For the wages of sin is death, but the gift of God is eternal life in Christ Jesus our Lord.   Romans 6:23

Second, the notion that there could be a sin for which the blood sacrifice of Jesus Christ was insufficient would be contradictory, since it would actually make sin more powerful than the cross. Paul said that where sin abounds grace abounds much more.

Moreover the law entered that the offense might abound. But where sin abounded, grace abounded much more, so that as sin reigned in death, even so grace might reign through righteousness to eternal life through Jesus Christ our Lord. Romans 5:20–21

Third, if it were true that there could exist sin that was greater than the blood sacrifice of Jesus Christ, He would have never resurrected from the dead. His resurrection from the dead was proof that His atonement was indeed greater than all the sin of the world—past present and future.

> Blessed be the God and Father of our Lord Jesus Christ, who according to His abundant mercy has begotten us again to a living hope through the resurrection of Jesus Christ from the dead, to an inheritance incorruptible and undefiled and that does not fade away, reserved in heaven for you, who are kept by the power of God through faith for salvation ready to be revealed in the last time. 1 Peter 1:3–5

Fourth, neither Paul the theologian of the New Testament, nor John whose text we are now considering recognized levels of sin. While it may be true that in the Old Testament sinful acts committed against individuals required various forms of retribution, this was probably for the benefit of those on the receiving end of injustice. However, as a whole, sin was not measured by the level of impact it had on people, but on the fact that it violated the holiness of God's character. Therefore, the smallest sin in comparison to the greatest sin still fell short of God's perfection.

Salvation is not God overlooking little sins and then applying the work of Calvary to the bigger sins. All sin is worthy of death; there are no sins less deserving of death unless you marginalize the holiness of God. The point is clear, sin no matter how small it may seem in the eyes of man, still separates us from God and separation from God is death. No one can stand worthy before God even if he considers his sins to be of a lesser degree. The reason Christ had to die was for the purpose of making atonement for all sin. In an effort to bring more light into the question of the unforgivable sin, John said the following:

> My little children, these things I write to you, so that you may not sin. And if anyone sins, we have an

166

Advocate with the Father, Jesus Christ the righteous.

1 John 2:1

In light of this verse, how is it possible that the sin committed in 1 John 5:16 was not within reach of the advocacy for the sin committed in 1 John 2:1? What is the difference between the sin committed in 2:1 for which there is advocacy, and the sin committed in 5:16 for which there is no advocacy? What can we say about a sin for which there is no forgiveness, and even more important, what is the wretched sin itself? I think every Christian would like to know in order to stay clearly away from it. Unfortunately, John does not tell us — or does he? We know that the unforgivable sin was not some grotesque immorality because there is no mention of any specific sin throughout the whole letter. What is clear in the letter of John is that he was writing to correct the false teachings of the Gnostics who were denying the complete personhood of Jesus Christ.

Jesus said that all sin was forgivable except blasphemy against the Holy Spirit (Mark 3:28–29). In the context of that warning two things stand out. First, Jesus was pointing to the religious leaders' lack of faith in Him as they were ascribing the authority of His ministry to Satan. This kind of reasoning showed a complete denial of faith in Christ's work of redemption. To deny Christ was to deny God's only means of salvation and die in a state of sin without hope. The second thing that appears clear regarding the unforgivable sin is that Christians cannot commit this sin, since we have already accepted God's condition for salvation.

We can grieve and quench the Holy Spirit—obviously not something we want to do—but we can never commit the unforgivable sin—blaspheme against the Holy Spirit. In light of the fact that Jesus said there is only one sin that cannot be forgiven, it is extremely unlikely that John was introducing a second sin for which there is no forgiveness and for which Christ Himself forgot to tell us about.

The purpose of John's writing was to combat the rise of Gnosticism and to give Christians a clear understanding of what it meant to be in true fellowship with God and Jesus Christ. Apparently, the efforts of Gnosticism were driven out and the true Christians remained faithful in this test. John made reference to a group of people who had deserted them.

> They went out from us, but they were not of us; for if they had been of us, they would have continued with us; but they went out that they might be made manifest, that none of them were of us.   1 John 2:19

It appears that what John had in mind in 5:16 has more similarity to what Jesus Himself said about blasphemy against the Holy Spirit. The only serious thing going on in the community of believers, was the false teaching of the Gnostics who denied the true nature of Jesus Christ. To interpret 1 John 5:16 as a verse that indicates a Christian can lose his salvation is forcing John to say what he is not saying at all. It is clear by the context of the letter that the sin unto death was not some gross act of sin that was greater than the atonement of Jesus Christ, but rather the sin of denying Christ as the only means of forgiveness.

John said in 1 John 5:17, "All unrighteousness is sin." At this point John was not making a distinction between deadly and un-deadly sin, all sin leads to death. In the same verse he says, "and there is sin not leading to death." Which are the sins that don't lead to death? They are the ones covered by the propitiation of Christ.

> My little children, these things I write to you, so that
> you may not sin. And if anyone sins, we have an
> Advocate with the Father, Jesus Christ the righteous.
> And He Himself is the propitiation for our sins, and
> not for ours only but also for the whole world.
>
> > 1 John 2:1–2

Which then, is the sin that leads to death without resolution? The whole context of John's letter would indicate that it is the same sin that Jesus said there was no forgiveness for—blasphemy against the Holy Spirit. John is not introducing a second sin for which there is no forgiveness; there is only one unforgivable sin, and both Jesus Christ and the apostle John are in agreement on what it is. There is no need for endless speculation for this reason John says:

> By this you know the Spirit of God: Every spirit that
> confesses that Jesus Christ has come in the flesh is of
> God, and every spirit that does not confess that Jesus
> Christ has come in the flesh is not of God. And this
> is the spirit of the Antichrist, which you have heard
> was coming, and is now already in the world.
>
> > 1 John 4:2–3

John continues to say in chapter 5 verse 18 that those who are truly born of God do not fall under the deception of the wicked one, but remain true to what God has revealed to us through Jesus Christ.

> We know that whoever is born of God does not sin;
> but he who has been born of God keeps himself, and
> the wicked one does not touch him. We know that we
> are of God, and the whole world lies under the sway
> of the wicked one. And we know that the Son of God

has come and has given us an understanding, that we
may know Him who is true; and we are in Him who
is true, in His Son Jesus Christ. This is the true God
and eternal life.   1 John 5:18–20

As John concludes his letter, his final words of encouragement
regard keeping themselves from idols. Once again proving that
there was no evidence for some gross immorality that would have
necessitated sudden judgment from God. It is clear that the sin unto
death was the denial of Jesus Christ as the only means for salvation.

Little children, keep yourselves from idols. Amen.
                                                1 John 5:21

I Will Not Blot His Name From the Book of Life

He who overcomes shall be clothed in white garments, and I will not blot out his name from the Book
of Life; but I will confess his name before My Father
and before His angels.   Revelation 3:5

This verse in the book of Revelation is also among the quoted
texts which is interpreted as a possibility for losing salvation. In this
particular interpretation, it becomes clear that; although it is God who
initiates salvation, staying saved is determined by the efforts of man.

If it is true that this verse is positively stating one can actually
lose their salvation, then salvation as a whole cannot be strictly by
grace alone. At best, it is a combination of grace plus works. For
reasons unknown to us, God is strong enough to initiate salvation,
but not strong enough to see it all the way through.

Man, whom the apostle Paul declared a sinner and fallen short of God's glory and who himself admitted that there was nothing good in his flesh, is elevated to the position of co-redeemer. God initiates redemption, but it is up to man to keep and finish what God started. The idea of man being in a co-redemptive partnership with God is blasphemous and contradicts the whole message of salvation in both the Old and New Testament. Paul's message to the Philippians was exceptionally clear.

> Being confident of this very thing, that He who has begun a good work in you will complete it until the day of Jesus Christ.   Philippians 1:6

For those who interpret this verse as a possibility for losing salvation, the promise of eternal life in John 3:16 is ultimately contingent on man's strength not in the power of the blood of the Lamb. In this respect the conclusion is obvious; you better overcome, or else you will die in your sin and lose your salvation. Perhaps the scariest thought for the honest seeker is the fact that, if indeed, we must all overcome by our own strength, then in the end no one will ever really be saved. I can't imagine anyone with integrity claiming they can live up to God's standards on any consistent basis without God's help through the Holy Spirit. Wasn't this the heart cry of the apostle Paul?

> For the good that I will *to do,* I do not do; but the evil I will not *to do,* that I practice.   Romans 7:19

The Christian life is impossible to live without the help of the Holy Spirit who is given to us under the grace covenant. Jesus Christ Himself said we could do nothing without Him (John 15:5). A salvation that is kept on the basis of human effort makes a mockery of the life, death, and resurrection of Jesus Christ. I am not stronger than Jesus Christ and neither are you, stop kidding yourself.

The other interpretation of this verse is to see it as an affirmation that those who overcome through faith in Jesus Christ have the assurance of eternal security and their names will never be erased from the Book of Life. The fact that there are two contradictory views regarding the meaning of this verse makes it obvious that the issue of eternal security or the lack of eternal security

A salvation that is kept on the basis of human effort makes a mockery of the life, death, and resurrection of Jesus Christ

cannot rest on this one verse alone. This fifty-fifty debate can last until we all turn blue in the face.

For this reason, the issue of eternal security must rest on what we believe is the meaning of Christ's holy life; His substitutionary death, His resurrection, and His intercessory prayer on behalf of the saints. The same John who wrote the book of Revelation said in the Gospel that bears his name that becoming a son or daughter of God is not the result of human effort or merit.

> But as many as received Him, to them He gave the right to become children of God, to those who believe in His name: who were born, not of blood, nor of the will of the flesh, nor of the will of man, but of God. John 1:12–13

John himself said in the book of Revelation nine chapters later, that they who overcame did so through the blood of the Lamb.

Then I heard a loud voice saying in heaven, "Now salvation, and strength, and the kingdom of our God, and the power of His Christ have come, for the accuser of our brethren, who accused them before our God day and night, has been cast down. And they overcame him by the blood of the Lamb and by the word of their testimony, and they did not love their lives to the death.   Revelation 12:10–11

Living as Overcomers

Any notion that salvation is God's grace plus man's works is not New Testament salvation. However, it should be noted that all seven churches in Revelation 2–3 were given admonitions to live as overcomers.

- To the church at Ephesus, Christ said that those who overcame would be given to eat from the tree of life that is in the paradise of God (Revelation 2:7).

- To the church at Smyrna, Christ said the overcomer would not be hurt by the second death (Revelation 2:11).

- To the church at Pergamos, Christ said the overcomer would be given to eat hidden manna and a white stone upon which a new name would be written (Revelation 2:17).

- To the church of Thyatira, Christ said those who overcame would be given power to rule over nations (Revelation 2:26).

- To the church at Sardis, Christ said the overcomers would be clothed in white garments, and their names would not be blotted out of the Book of Life, but confessed before God and His angels (Revelation 3:5).

- To the church at Philadelphia, Christ said the overcomers would be made pillars in the temple of God, and the name of God and the name of God's city would be written on them. Additionally, Christ's new name would also be written on them. (Revelation 3:12).

- To the church at Laodicea, Christ said the overcomers would be granted to sit with Him on His throne (Revelation 3:21).

It would be extremely difficult to justify an interpretation that would make believers responsible for overcoming sin by their own strength in order to maintain their salvation. In Romans chapter seven, the apostle Paul gave conclusive evidence that mankind in his own strength is in a wretched hopeless state.

> O wretched man that I am! Who will deliver me from
> this body of death?   Romans 7:24

It is clear that the messages given to these churches in regard to overcoming were a reference to eternal rewards not eternal security. There is really no other alternate interpretation that would be credible. However, since they were admonished to live as overcomers, what does it actually mean to be an overcomer? And most important, were they expected to overcome through their own efforts, or were they expected to overcome on Christ's provision for victory? It is very interesting that in all of the seven messages given to the churches, Christ revealed Himself in the way that corresponded directly with the issues they were struggling with.

Overcoming at Ephesus

To the church at Ephesus who had lost their first love, Christ revealed Himself as the one who walked in their midst. If they had lost their intimacy with Christ it wasn't that Christ had moved away from them, but that they had moved away from Him. In Christian life, it is not impossible to replace practicing the presence of Jesus with a commitment to practicing activities.

Not that these things are wrong in themselves; however, the power source in Christian living is not in activities or good principles, but in spending time with Jesus Christ. The motivation to repent (change of mind-set) and do the first works came from the fact that Christ had not left His servant nor His church. In the final analysis, Christ's love for the messenger and the church had not diminished after the passing of time. They could overcome their declining fervency by remembering that Christ was still fervently in love with them and missed the intimacy He had enjoyed with them in the past. Losing sight of God's closeness is our greatest downfall.

Overcoming at Smyrna

To the church at Smyrna, Christ said that the death challenges they faced could be overcome by remembering that Christ Himself was the First and the Last, the one who had been dead and had come back to life again. In light of this truth, they could overcome the fear of physical death by remembering that eternal death would not have any claim on their lives (Revelation 2:8).

Overcoming at Pergamos

To the church at Pergamos who was struggling with issues of doctrinal purity, Christ revealed Himself as the one with the sharp two-edged sword. They could overcome the infiltration of false doctrine by staying true to God's Word (Revelation 2:12).

Overcoming at Thyatira

To the church at Thyatira who was struggling with issues of immorality, Christ revealed Himself as the one with eyes like a flame of fire and feet like fine brass. Their overcoming immorality would obviously result from refocusing on God's holiness and remembering that Christ was the true pattern for life (Revelation 2:18).

Overcoming at Sardis

To the church at Sardis who was spiritually dead, Christ revealed Himself as the one who had the seven Spirits of God and the seven stars. Their overcoming would result from repenting and by reinstating Christ in their hearts who already had them in His right hand. They needed an all out revival and to re-establish themselves in the things they had received and heard in previous days when they were spiritually alive (Revelation 3:1, 3).

Overcoming at Philadelphia

No apparent failure was noted in the church of Philadelphia. Nevertheless, Christ revealed Himself as the one who is holy and true, who has the key of David, and who opens doors no one can shut. Perhaps they just needed some affirmation to continue faithfully (Revelation 3:7–8).

Overcoming at Laodicea

To the lukewarm church of the Laodiceans who appeared to have no truth on which to stand on for anything, Christ revealed Himself as the ultimate truth. He is the Amen, the True Witness, the Beginning of the creation of God. Apparently, the church had become satisfied with what the world had to offer more than they were concerned with being His witnesses to a lost world. Christ said that although they appeared to be lacking nothing, in reality they were wretched, miserable, poor, blind, and naked. Christ bids them to come and buy from Him the true riches of life. Their overcoming would result from seeing Christ for who He truly is, something that they had lost touch with (Revelation 3:14–18).

What Is the Meaning in These Messages?

From what we have seen so far, it is obvious that the admonition to overcome would not rest on their own strength, but on the fact that Christ Himself was the provision for their overcoming victory. This is the reason why Christ the Lord revealed Himself in specific correlation to what each church needed. Without Christ being who He was in relationship to what each church needed, overcoming would be impossible.

The apostle Paul in addressing the Corinthians provides a parallel to what we have just seen in Revelation. Paul said that God would not allow the Christians at Corinth to be tempted above what they were able to handle, but that in the temptation, God would be faithful to provide a way for them to escape and bear it. Their overcoming victory would not stand on the strength of the Corinthians nor on the practice of positive thinking—"I think I can," "I know I can," "I will I can,"—but on the faithfulness of God Himself.

> No temptation has overtaken you except such as is
> common to man; but God is faithful, who will not
> allow you to be tempted beyond what you are able,
> but with the temptation will also make the way of
> escape, that you may be able to bear it.
>
> 1 Corinthians 10:13

Standing and Works

> For by grace you have been saved through faith, and
> that not of yourselves; *it is* the gift of God, not of
> works, lest anyone should boast. For we are His work-
> manship, created in Christ Jesus for good works,
> which God prepared beforehand that we should walk
> in them.   Ephesians 2:8-10

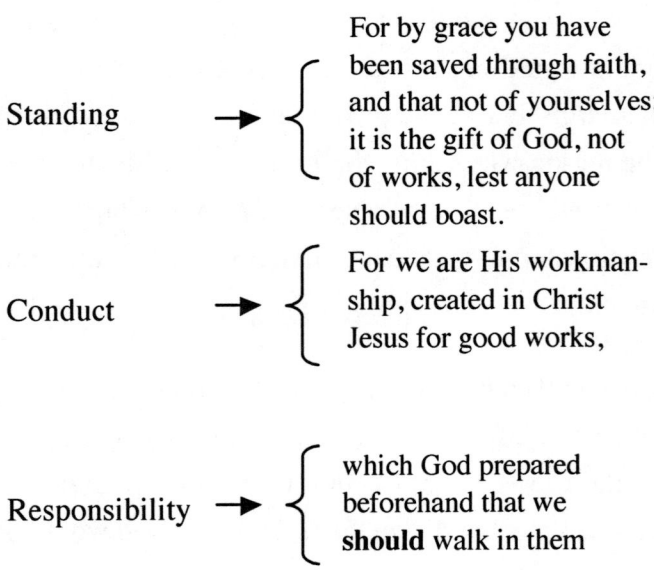

Standing → For by grace you have been saved through faith, and that not of yourselves; it is the gift of God, not of works, lest anyone should boast.

Conduct → For we are His workmanship, created in Christ Jesus for good works,

Responsibility → which God prepared beforehand that we **should** walk in them

In the messages given to the seven leaders over the seven churches
in Revelation, it is very clear that the issue is concerning their *works*

in Christ, not their *standing* in Christ. After the preliminary address identifying the church to whom the message was written to, the formula that follows is the same for all seven churches. It begins with "I know your works." With regard to where they stood in relationship to their eternal security, Christ Himself answered this question in the first chapter.

> Regarding the mystery of the seven stars you saw in My right hand and of the seven golden lampstands: the seven stars are the heavenly messengers who preside over the seven churches, and the seven lampstands are the seven churches themselves.
>
> Revelation 1:20 VOICE

When Christ says, "I know your works," that is a reference to *conduct*, there is no room for any other interpretation. When Christ says He has the seven stars in His right hand, that is a reference to *standing*, there is no room for any other interpretation. *Standing* is what we have that is not derivative from human effort (therefore, we have saved by grace not works).

When Christ says, "I know your works," that is a reference to conduct; When Christ says He has the seven stars in His right hand, that is a reference to standing;

Conduct is what results from God working in our lives through grace (therefore, we have created in Jesus Christ for good works). *Responsibility* is realigning our lives to what is true of us from redemption rather than what is true of us from the fallen world (therefore, we have which God prepared beforehand that we *should* walk in).

Should in this context implies duty and responsibility, we should do good deeds. However, *should* also implies the possibility of not doing. It is important to know that *should* in this context is not a stand alone *should*, but stands on the fact that something has been done on our behalf that makes the *should* in the text more than a possibility, but a reality to be lived out. In other words, it is true that we are not saved nor kept by works, but works reflect the reality of our salvation.

In Christian living, new conduct always follows the understanding of new truth "The truth will set you free" (John 8:32). Being set free does not result from pure brute human effort. Paul has made this extremely clear in Romans: "For the good that I will to do, I do not do; but the evil I will not to do, that I practice" (Romans 7:19). Change in life comes from understanding truth and then realigning ourselves so that our lives are reflecting the new truth about us— redeemed in Christ. Truth not lived out is just as good as not knowing truth at all. For this reason, the Christian life could never be the result of pure human effort. One must be born again of the Holy Spirit.

Paul wrote to the Ephesians assuring them that their initial faith in Jesus Christ resulted in their being sealed with the Holy Spirit of promise. The Christian life cannot be lived out without the Holy Spirit because He is both the *illuminator of truth*; meaning He helps us understand truth, and He is the *power source of truth*, meaning He helps us to live out truth. This explains why salvation is the complete work of God independent of anything man can do. God willed salvation, Christ fulfilled salvation, and the Holy Spirit realizes it in our lives through the new birth. Through redemption we now have the privilege and what amounts to be the greatest blessing in life, to grow intimately with God because that door has now been opened. In Jesus priestly prayer recorded in John chapter 17, He prayed that we would be one with the Father as He is one with the Father (John 17:21).

What is extremely clear from the messages given to the seven churches in Revelation is that five of the seven churches had forgotten the truth they had been planted in. And their conduct began to reflect it. What was the antidote to this downward progression? Repent, (change of mind) and return to living out of their true identity. But what would happen if they didn't repent, would they lose their salvation?

Christ's Enduring Love in the Midst of Declining Faithfulness

In Christ's rebuke to stir up His church back to where they needed to be, several things stand out. *First,* before things get really bad, Christ is always the one who takes the first step in restoring what needs to be made right again. It was not the church who came seeking Christ out of its waywardness, but Christ who came in love to plead with His church. Before judgment, there is always mercy and grace coming from true love.

Perhaps this was the reason that in all the messages given to the seven churches, Christ commended them for doing some things right. Obviously in His strong rebuke, Christ did not want to break their spirits, but only desired to get their attention and bring them back to where they needed to be. Even to the churches of Sardis and Laodicea, to whom Christ gave His harshest words of rebuke, He still affirmed His love for them. To the church at Sardis Christ said that He had them in His hand and that they needed to remember what they had received and heard and repent from their gross indifference.

> And to the angel of the church in Sardis write, "These
> things says He who has the seven Spirits of God and
> the seven stars: 'I know your works, that you have a
> name that you are alive, but you are dead.''
>
> Revelation 3:1

Hearing a message that still affirmed His love for them in spite of their disobedience would have been encouraging enough for them to heed the call to repent. To the church at Laodicea, to whom Christ said He would vomit out of His mouth because they were neither cold nor hot. Christ finished His sermon by assuring them that if they heard His knock and voice, He would dine with them and they would sit with Him on his throne. There is a drastic difference between wanting to vomit the church out of His mouth and dining with them in intimacy.

His love for us always proves to be greater than our unwarranted disobedience towards Him. It is not judgment He wants to give us, but forgiveness and restoration.

> Behold, I stand at the door and knock. If anyone hears
> My voice and opens the door, I will come in to him
> and dine with him, and he with Me. To him who over-
> comes I will grant to sit with Me on My throne, as I
> also overcame and sat down with My Father on His
> throne.   Revelation 3:20–21

Second, what were the results that followed from the Lord's calling them to repentance? Did the church at Sardis and Laodicea repent as well as the others? Was it followed by a strong outpouring of revival? Well, we don't know; we are not given the history of what happened afterwards, at least not from Scripture. However, it is extremely inconceivable to think that after such strong warnings coming from the greatest love and promises of rewards, that they did not heed the call to repent.

Surely the church at Sardis would not have continued in its spiritual state of deadness once they had been exposed, not only because God knew their true state of affairs, but also because they must have felt extremely wretched in their shallow relationship with the Creator of the universe.

The same could be said of the church at Laodicea. How could they continue in their condition described as wretched, miserable, poor, blind, and naked, when the opportunity to make things right came from the appeal of a loving Lord and Savior? It is extremely difficult to believe that they refused what was brought before them. Nevertheless, for the sake of leaving no unturned stones, let's imagine a *third* possibility. What would have happened if after the warning given to the leaders and their respective churches they still refused to repent? Would they lose their salvation?

Paul's first letter written to the Corinthians provides some insight into what might occur in the lives of unrepentant sons and daughters of God. Paul said in chapter 11 that some of the believers were weak, others were sick, and many were sleeping (1 Corinthians 11:30). Take notice of the word *many*. Many were sleeping; the sleeping mentioned here was not a reference to taking a power nap. The word *many sleep* literally means that they had died. The chastisement surrounding the disorderly conduct in observing the Lord's Supper included different levels of discipline, including death. In light of this very strong judgment, it is necessary to take notice of what death means from a Christian perspective. Although it is true that in this particular case, death was a means of judgment. Nevertheless, the analogy of seeing death as being asleep is not something horrific that should be dreaded and avoided as long as we possibly can. People that sleep do so to replenish their strength and wake up renewed in the morning. This is the idea Paul communicated to the Thessalonians when referring to believers who had died in Christ.

> But I do not want you to be ignorant, brethren, concerning those who have fallen asleep, lest you sorrow as others who have no hope. For if we believe that Jesus died and rose again, even so God will bring with Him those who sleep in Jesus.   1 Thessalonians 4:13–14

Additionally, Paul said to the Corinthians that when believers are judged by the Lord, they are not condemned with the world.

> But when we are judged, we are chastened by the Lord, that we may not be condemned with the world.
> 1 Corinthians 11:32

So what is the answer to the question at hand? What happens to believers who refuse correction? According to 1 Corinthians, Christians who refuse correction are taken home. But since the ultimate goal of every Christian is to die in order to live better by being in God's presence, wouldn't death still have been a form of reward for the disobedient Corinthians? Not in the least, premature death robs us of God's intended destiny for us and robs us of the glory God would have received from our obedience. For this reason, Paul was always very conscious of God's calling on his life.

> Now this I do for the gospel's sake, that I may be partaker of it with you. Do you not know that those who run in a race all run, but one receives the prize? Run

in such a way that you may obtain it. And everyone
who competes for the prize is temperate in all things.
Now they do it to obtain a perishable crown, but we
for an imperishable crown. Therefore I run thus: not
with uncertainty. Thus I fight: not as one who beats
the air. But I discipline my body and bring it into subjection, lest, when I have preached to others, I myself
should become disqualified.   1 Corinthians 9:23–27

Obviously, for Paul the ambassador of grace, his mention of being
disqualified was not a reference to losing salvation, but a reference to
a disciplined life that allowed him to be used for the glory of God. His
life was the exact opposite of what was happening in five of the seven
churches addressed in the book of Revelation. His all out desire was
to be a vessel that would bring honor to God. He considered no other
purpose in life higher than the calling on his life. This gratitude and
intensity for God's purpose were what had weakened in five of the
seven churches in Revelation. The same sentiment was encouraged
in Paul's letter to Timothy.

You therefore must endure hardship as a good soldier
of Jesus Christ. No one engaged in warfare entangles
himself with the affairs of this life, that he may please
him who enlisted him as a soldier. 2 Timothy 2:3–4

What the Security and Hope of Believers Means in Everyday life

In a fallen world we all know the experience of suffering and pain;
whether through the loss of a loved one, a personal crisis, injustice at
the hands of other human beings, or just the everyday heartbreak of a
love relationship gone wrong. It is impossible not to cross paths with

the brokenness of the world. In ministry, I often encounter people who feel like God doesn't love them pointing to their circumstances. God's ultimate love for us cannot be measured by the consequences that sin has brought upon all of us. Rather, God's love for us can be fully validated by what He did in spite of our rebellion. For this reason Paul said:

> But God demonstrates His own love toward us, in that while we were still sinners, Christ died for us.
>
> Romans 5:8

The suffering we experience in life is not the result of God not loving us, but rather the result of a fallen world caused by Adam and Eve's disobedience. They are responsible for the brokenness we all experience and the reason why we sometimes falsely accuse God of not loving us. God created Paradise, Adam and Eve slaughtered paradise. We inherited Adam and Eve's sin nature that rebels against God, but God promises to restore paradise. There is no need for misplaced blame. If you want to blame God accurately, blame Him for loving us in spite of our choosing to rebel against His bountiful grace in the Garden of Eden and for providing a redemption that cost Him His only begotten Son. For those who constantly complain that life is not fair, I say you are correct. In a fallen world life is never fair. But since we are on the subject of unfairness, consider the life of Jesus Christ. Why did He have to suffer and die? He was never in any rebellion towards God. There was never any sin in Him.

It should be apparent that we are not the greatest sufferers of injustice, the greatest sufferer of injustice was the Son of God Himself. He left heaven to come into a broken world and live among sinners, experiencing rejection, temptation, and hunger and acquainting Himself with every kind of human suffering. He wept for the human condition and in response to it chose to die for sin that was not His own, so that we could stand again in right relationship with God.

No human suffering can compare with His. I am not trying to minimize your own personal suffering, we all feel the pain from living in a fallen world. Nevertheless, we should never lose sight of the fact that it was precisely our suffering and pain, caused by our own sin that He chose a crown of thorns, the cross, and the nails.

> We despised him and rejected him—a man of sorrows, acquainted with bitterest grief. We turned our backs on him and looked the other way when he went by. He was despised, and we didn't care. Yet it was our grief he bore, our sorrows that weighed him down. And we thought his troubles were a punishment from God, for his own sins! But he was wounded and bruised for our sins. He was beaten that we might have peace; he was lashed—and we were healed!   Isaiah 53:3–5 TLB

The cross becomes our turning point in life—the end to a life without hope and the beginning of a life journey in which Christ is our companion; who redeems, restores, comforts, guides, and promises to make all things new. For this reason, the brokenness and injustice we all experience from time to time cannot be viewed as our greatest setback in life. The greatest setback in life is always in not seeing God's greatest love demonstrated on the cross. That will always create the greatest suffering and injustice in our

The cross becomes our turning point in life—the end to a life without hope and the beginning of a life journey in which Christ is our companion who redeems, restores, comforts, guides, and promises to make all things new.

lives, because through it we remain stuck in our own pool of Bethesda (John 5:2–8).

God values our lives. He wants to bring restoration into our lives, the cross is proof of that. God has not abandoned us in our rebellion, He has not forgotten us in our suffering, and He is not indifferent towards our emotional heartbreaks. God promises to make all things new.

> Now I saw a new heaven and a new earth, for the first heaven and the first earth had passed away. Also there was no more sea. Then I, John, saw the holy city, New Jerusalem, coming down out of heaven from God, prepared as a bride adorned for her husband. And I heard a loud voice from heaven saying, "Behold, the tabernacle of God is with men, and He will dwell with them, and they shall be His people. God Himself will be with them and be their God. And God will wipe away every tear from their eyes; there shall be no more death, nor sorrow, nor crying. There shall be no more pain, for the former things have passed away." Then He who sat on the throne said, "Behold, I make all things new." And He said to me, "Write, for these words are true and faithful."   Revelation 21:1–5

In a world like ours, the hope we have in God is the ultimate source of strength and courage as we walk through the valley of a broken world. "When trapped in a tunnel of misery, hope points to the light at the end.

When we struggle with a crippling disease or a lingering illness, hope helps us persevere beyond the pain. When we fear the worst, hope brings reminders that God is still in control. Simply put, when life hurts, and dreams fade, nothing helps like hope."[13]

"Humans strive to understand and achieve a meaningful picture of their world. Otherwise we would have no basis for evaluating new situations and choosing corrective actions. Unless we can see order and predictability in our environment, we cannot work out an intelligent response to life."[14] Through the redemption that is in Christ Jesus, we have the hope that allows us to work out an intelligent response to life. We are able to live life with the expectation of a new world where our greatest hopes will all be realized and all our wounds will all be completely healed.

For all of the redeemed in Christ, we have this blessed assurance that in the end, God wins, and His victory will be our victory too. I am sure you hate living in a fallen world, as we all do, but in Christ we have this assurance that God will make all things new. He will wipe away every tear, He will heal every disease, and heal every broken heart. He will make every wrong right, evil will be no more for this reason Paul said in Romans:

> For I consider that the sufferings of this present time
> are not worthy to be compared with the glory which
> shall be revealed in us.   Romans 8:18

Epilogue

Staying on Course

It has been my experience in ministry that many Christians have failed to understand and master what is at the core of Christian spirituality. While many may have initially embraced the love and forgiveness of God, a shallow understanding of His redemption leads to living with uncertainty and devoid of the growth, peace, and joy that comes from the truth that sets us free. The apostle Paul said righteousness, peace, and joy are the common characteristics of Christian living on this side of heaven (Romans 14:17). There is a great need today for believers in Christ to master the meaning of redemption. In fact, my motivation for writing a book like this comes from listening to people who want to thrive in their relationship with God, but who always end up feeling defeated and unworthy before their Creator God. When God's people fail to clearly understand how redemption unfolds in their lives they will slow down the process of sanctification, get stuck in continual repentance without growth, or just drop out completely. Through years of pastoral counseling I have observed that people who don't master the meaning of redemption tend to drop out of church in four stages.

The Stage of Frustration

In the first stage, *the stage of frustration,* there is a struggle in the mind of the believer between the idealism of God's holiness and the reality that none of us have arrived. Obviously for those who are truly born again, behavior and conduct become very important factors in Christian living. For genuine believers, there is no reason to doubt that the new mind-set is one in which they seek to kill sin in their lives, just as sin seeks to kill them. The struggle between God's holiness and the reality of our fallen nature is one the apostle Paul described in detail in Romans chapter 7. His purpose in writing was not to break our spirit and leave us in complete hopelessness; rather, it was to show us that God has made another way. Jesus Christ has become the new law of grace by which we stand fully accepted in God's presence. While it is true that we still struggle, the greater truth is that we are not struggling to be accepted by God, but we struggle because we have been eternally accepted by God.

In the daily life of a Christian there must be a clear distinction between **standing** and **conduct**. Standing is what we have already secured through what Jesus Christ accomplished on the cross. It was a onetime event in history and will never be repeated nor is it subject to change for all eternity, this is our justification. Justification means that God sees us through Christ's righteousness not through our own fallen sin nature. Conduct, on the other hand is not an event, but a continual work in progress in which we are being transformed into the likeness of Christ through the ongoing work of the Holy Spirit. This work continues for the duration of our life, it is our sanctification. Failure to make this distinction early in Christian life results in applying what Christ accomplished for us in reverse order. In reverse order, what we attempt to do is to make our *conduct* (sanctification) the basis of how we stand before God, rather than *Christ's conduct* (justification), what He accomplished at the cross.

Why does this happen so often in the lives of believers? The primary reason I believe this happens is that every single day of our lives it is our conduct (sanctification) that we see. Our standing (justification) cannot be seen with physical eyes because that event happened over 2000 years ago, we were not there and it must be embraced as an act of faith. While it is true that through Christ, God no longer sees our fallen nature, we, on the other hand still see and feel our daily bloopers.

Herein lies the challenge, to acknowledge everyday *conduct* there is no effort needed, all we need is our physical eyes wide open. But to acknowledge our *standing*, that cannot be seen with our physical eyes, we need the effort of the mind in order to see it. This visualization of the mind is what amounts to the Christian faith. Faith implies trust; faith says, "I don't see it but I trust in believing it is true." In Hebrews 11, we have a history of people who practiced this visualization of the mind. They again and again trusted in what they could not see with their physical eyes and moved toward what God had promised them by faith.

> Now faith is the substance of things hoped for, the
> evidence of things not seen.   Hebrews 11:1

If every day we could see with our physical eyes Christ being crucified on our behalf, the error we so easily fall into of putting *conduct* (what we see with our eyes) before *standing* (what is received by faith) would be dramatically neutralized, if not nonexistent. However, we all know this isn't going to happen just for our convenience, but it doesn't take away from the fact that it did happen. It happened as a one-time event to impact the outcome of how people would stand before God for all eternity, and we are called to believe it and commit our eternal security and destiny to this very truth.

> For in it the righteousness of God is revealed from faith to faith; as it is written, "The just shall live by faith." [not by conduct].   Romans 1:17

The Lord Jesus Christ, however, *did* establish something that would help us with the visualization of His crucifixion when He instituted the Lord's Supper. In the Lord's Supper, we have a symbolic but nevertheless physical eye seeing observation of what He accomplished for us at Calvary. The bread is a reminder to us of His body that suffered on our behalf. The wine is the reminder of His blood that was shed for the remission of sins and is the basis of the new covenant between God and man.

The Stage of Discouragement

If we continue to live in reverse order by making our conduct the basis of how we stand before God, it will only create uncertainty as we are all very much aware of our own shortcomings. When there is confusion between our right standing with God, that which was accomplished through the death of Christ as a onetime event (justification), and our conduct (sanctification), that which is ongoing throughout the duration of life, the result most often will lead to discouragement. In the stage of discouragement, there is a continual on-and-off uncertainty about how one stands with God (He loves me, He loves me not). Individuals experiencing this stage often carry a burden of thoughts that no one else sees or hears and that often result in self-condemnation and isolation. Everyone knows from personal life experiences that nothing defeats the motivation in the human heart more than to experience failure and then to feel rejected on the basis of that failure.

The opposite of course; is just as true, nothing motivates the hearts of human beings more than to know that after they have failed, God will not fail them. He will never give up on them, nor will He abandon them or see them with a lesser degree of love. In fact, the very reason we were all driven to the gospel in the first place was this triumph of love over failure—this amazing grace, how sweet it is. Yes, on the cross, God's love was stronger than sin—stronger than all our past, present, and future failures.

> Moreover the law entered that the offense might
> abound. But where sin abounded, grace abounded
> much more.   Romans 5:20

The Stage of Disillusionment

In the *stage of disillusionment,* serious doubts will be entertained in our minds concerning the validity of our faith. The inward conversation may resemble one of the following scenarios:

Scenario #1
I am a Christian and I struggle. Therefore, I must not be a true Christian, because if I were a true Christian I would not struggle.

Scenario #2
I am a Christian and I struggle. Therefore, Christianity must not be true because it didn't deliver what it promised.

The truth, however about being alive in Christ is that it is a struggle. Unfortunately, the very struggle that validates our spiritual authenticity is often interpreted as spiritual defeat rather than spiritual reality. To struggle means that you are alive, only the dead cease to struggle. The disciple of Christ has been called to a life of spiritual warfare. We are in a struggle with a fallen creature (Satan) who comes to tempt and accuse us. We are in a struggle with a fallen world system whose ideology is to seek value, purpose, and meaning outside of a relationship with God. We are in a struggle with a fallen sinful nature that manifests itself in a lifestyle that seeks its own way of fulfillment rather than to trust in the goodness of the fatherhood of God.

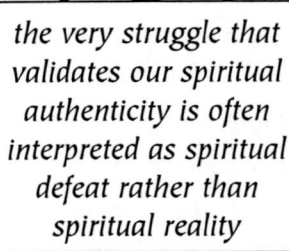

the very struggle that validates our spiritual authenticity is often interpreted as spiritual defeat rather than spiritual reality

At this point, however, we must be encouraged by knowing that we are not alone in this struggle. We have been equipped for victory. When the accuser comes to bombard us with accusations of wrong doing which for the most part will unfortunately be true, we have the righteousness of Christ in response to his faultfinding. When the ideology of the world seeks to conform us and make us one of its own, we have the truth of God as our lie-detection system by which we measure truth from error. When the flesh is weak and seeks the easy way out, we have the Holy Spirit as our internal support system, empowering us to victory and reminding us of His promises by which we look forward to a better future. When we feel discouraged, we have an external support system in the body of believers through which we find mutual comfort and edification. We are not alone in our struggle, but more important is knowing beyond a shadow of a doubt that the struggle we are in, is not to determine how we will ultimately stand before God in the end. That struggle has already been won at the cross where Christ Himself declared it finished. The struggle in Christian life is not with how we stand, but how we walk.

Ironically, in living the Christian life victoriously, knowing how we already stand is the foundation that determines how we walk in victory. If new believers, or even mature believers in Christ, fail to understand where their true struggle lies, they will focus all their energy on working to be good enough to be accepted by God. This futile exercise of the flesh is what Paul experienced as a coming to the end of himself in chapter 7 of Romans. It is the same coming to the end of self that every New Testament Christian must experience for himself if he is going to position himself for real sanctification in the Holy Spirit. Without this awareness the ultimate place we all land is in the stage of abandonment, as we conclude we can't win. And we are correct—we can't win by our own strength. That is the clear reason Jesus Christ needed to come to earth, to die and resurrect from the dead so that our victory would ultimately stand on what He accomplished and not on human effort.

The Stage of Abandonment

In the last stage, the *stage of abandonment* the cycle is completed. A decision will be made to put God on hold and leave the relationship with Him for a later time. In the worst-case scenario, it's possible to just walk away completely or begin a new spiritual search—one that fits your human capacity, one that you can control, one that you can turn on and off at your convenience.

That is what religion is all about. It does not require a growing, intimate relationship with God, it only requires religious activities without a change of heart. This is what the New Testament Pharisees had; religion without relationship, and it manifested itself in attitudes and behaviors that did not fit real-life situations. They kept their hands washed but failed to have mercy in their hearts.

Staying in the Process

The focus of this book has clearly been to help you master the meaning of redemption as it unfolds in your life as a four-part process of one single truth. You will never get just one part of redemption — you get all four parts. Each one has a different function. In justification, God accepts you eternally. In sanctification, God begins to transform your life through the work of the Holy Spirit giving you the ultimate extreme makeover. In calling, God redeems your future giving you a new reference point to the past. You become an extension of His kingdom purposes to share your redemption story with the world. In God's eternal security, you are kept under His protection which ultimately leads to your glorification, the end of experiencing life in a fallen world and the beginning of an eternity with God. Staying in this process depends upon knowing that God loves you eternally, He will never leave you and everything God promises to do in your life is based upon what Jesus Christ has already accomplished through His life, death, resurrection and priestly intercession. His redemption unfolding in your life is truly life's greatest adventure, for this reason our Lord Jesus said:

> Again, the kingdom of heaven is like treasure hidden in a field, which a man found and hid; and for joy over it he goes and sells all that he has and buys that field.   Matthew 13:44

To the Father, Son, and the Holy Spirit be all
the glory and honor who is able
to redeem completely from sin and death.

Notes

Chapter 1

Chip Ingram, *God: As He Longs for You to See Him* (Grand Rapids, MI: Baker Books 2007), 20.

Chapter 3

Myles Munroe, *Understanding the Purpose and Power of Men* (New Kensington, PA: Whitaker House 2001), 42.

Robert Jeffress, *Guilt Free Living* (Wheaton, IL: Tyndale House Publishers, INC., 1995), 95.

Joseph M. Stowell, *Following Christ* (Grand Rapids, MI: Zondervan Publishing House, 1996), 27.

Chapter 4

David G. Benner, *Surrender to Love* (Downers Grove, IL: InterVarsity Press 2003), 11.

Chapter 5

John R. W. Stott, *Baptism and Fullness* (Downers Grove, IL: InterVarsity Press, 1975), 20.

Chapter 6

Erik Rees, *S.H.A.P.E.: Finding and Fulfilling Your Unique Purpose for Life* (Grand Rapids, MI: Zondervan Publishing House, 2006), 22.

John Ortberg, *You Can't Take It with You* (Grand Rapids, MI: Zondervan Publishing House, 2009), 4.

John Ortberg, *You Can't Take it With You* (Grand Rapids, MI: Zondervan Publishing House 2009), 6.

Louie Giglio, *I Am Not But I Know I AM* (Colorado Springs, CO: Multnomah Books, 2005), 9

Myles Munroe, *Releasing Your Potential* (Shippensburg, PA: Destiny Image Publishers, Inc., 2007), 24.

Myles Munroe, *Releasing Your Potential* (Shippensburg PA.: Destiny Image Publishers, INC. 2007), 40.

Chapter 7

Charles R. Swindoll, *Hope Again: When Life Hurts and Dreams Fade* (Dallas, London, Vancouver, Melbourne: Word Publishing, 1996), xi–xii.

James C. Coleman, James N. Butcher, Robert C. Carson, *Abnormal Psychology,* 7th ed. (Dallas: Scott Foresman and Company, 1984), 112.

CPSIA information can be obtained
at www.ICGtesting.com
Printed in the USA
FSOW01n2119171115
13539FS

9 781498 439893